In Memory of

Walter Roscoe

Presented by

Mr. & Mrs. Edward Susi
Mr. & Mrs. Scott Griffith

A CONCISE GUIDE TO GAME SHOOTING

A CONCISE GUIDE TO GAME SHOOTING

Michael Brander

·THE·
SPORTSMAN'S
PRESS
LONDON

This edition published in 1986 by The Sportsman's Press.
This revised edition © Michael Brander 1988.
First published 1965 under the title
THE GAMESHOT'S VADE MECUM, reprinted 1971.
All Rights Reserved.

For
A.M.B.

British Library of Congress Cataloguing in Publication Data

Brander, Michael
  A concise guide to game shooting.—Rev. ed.
  1. Hunting—Great Britain
  I. Title   II. Brander, Michael. Game shot's
  vade mecum
  799.2'13'0941   SK185

  ISBN 0-948253-04-5

Printed and bound in Great Britain by
Redwood Burn Limited, Trowbridge, Wiltshire

CONTENTS

5

BOOK TWO

THE APPROACH TO SHOOTING

PART 1—THE INITIAL STEPS

PART 2—GUN HANDLING AND GUN SAFETY

ELEMENTARY STAGES

PART 3—PRELIMINARIES TO SHOOTING

PART 4—THE THEORY AND PRACTICE OF SHOOTING

A. MAINLY THEORETICAL

BOOK THREE

THE BACKGROUND OF SHOOTING

PART 1—WEATHER, SCENT, GAME BEHAVIOUR AND MARKING

PART 2—THE GAME

PART 3—THE ORGANISATION OF SHOOTING

PART 4—SHOOT MANAGEMENT

A. THE MOOR

B. PARTRIDGE GROUND

DRAWINGS IN THE TEXT

PREFACE

THIS book was first published in 1965 under the somewhat dated title *The Gameshot's Vade Mecum*, as a companion volume to Maunsell's *Fisherman's Vade Mecum*. A revised edition was printed in 1971. This updated edition still fills a gap in the market, since no other *Concise Guide* on these lines has been written and it remains a useful work of reference, especially for the novice shot. It is not intended to be read at a sitting. It is a collection of notes on most subjects connected with game shooting laid out in as convenient and logical a manner as possible to provide the game shot, especially the novice, with a guide to his sport. Although intended primarily for the general guidance of the beginner, there may be various points in it of interest to the more experienced shooting man as well. It should be appreciated, however, that the drawings are simply intended to illustrate points in the text and are not necessarily either to scale or accurate in detail.

INTRODUCTION

Preliminary Points to Remember

To GET the most from his sport the beginner should always realise:

i. While a knowledge of ballistics and theory is all very well the ability to shoot straight is infinitely more desirable and this can only be learned by practice. At the same time these are only two aspects of the many interests and satisfactions to be obtained from his sport.
ii. His sport should provide him with an interest in the countryside not merely during the shooting season, but throughout the year.
iii. This interest should extend not only to game birds and their predators, both in season and out, but also to all other aspects of nature and the countryside connected with them.
iv. Even if he is not a countryman himself it is desirable that he should accept the standards of the countryside and lend his support to other field sports.
v. The shotgun is a lethal weapon, far more deadly at close quarters than a rifle. EVERY SHOTGUN SHOULD BE TREATED AT ALL TIMES AS IF IT IS LOADED.

BOOK 1

The Mechanics of Shooting

PART I

THE SHOTGUN

A. *The Parts of the Gun*
(*A double-barrelled side by side*)

Section 1. The Barrels

The Barrels are the cylindrical steel tubes in which the cartridges are inserted and through which the shot charge travels when the gun is fired.

i. The length of the barrels must be greater than 24 inches or a Firearms Certificate is required by law.

ii. There is no maximum length, but for game shooting 30 inches

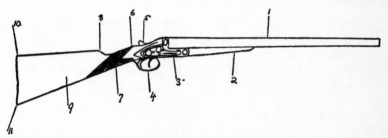

Fig. 1. Parts of the Gun

1. Barrel. 2. Fore-end. 3. Lock. 4. Trigger guard. 5. Top lever. 6. Safety catch. 7. Grip, hand, or small of butt. 8. Comb. 9. Stock. 10. Heel, or bump, of butt. 11. Toe of butt.

is the longest practical length in general use. At one time this was the commonest length for most shotguns.

iii. Although 25 and 26 inch barrels are common enough the most popular length today is 28 inches.

Section 2. The Bore

The Bore of a shotgun is the inside of the barrel above the cartridge chamber.

i. The size of a shotgun is gauged by the diameter of the bore.

B   17

ii. The classification is by the 'weight of the projectile' as in archaic gunnery when cannon were measured by the weight of the cannon balls in pounds, e.g. six pounder.

iii. The shotgun size is gauged by the number of pure lead spherical balls of a size exactly fitting the diameter of the bore which go to the pound, e.g. 12 bore, or 12 balls to the pound.

iv. The commonest bores, or gauges, for game shooting are as follows:

Size, or gauge, of bore	Average diameter of bore
12	·729 inch
16	·662
20	·615
28	·550

Any bore smaller than 32 is given by the measurement of the diameter in decimals. The best known is ·410.

Section 3. *The Parts of the Barrels*

i. The Chamber: is that part of the barrel slightly enlarged to receive the cartridge. Between it and the bore is the chamber cone, which is the tapered part connecting them. Looking through the barrel, this will be seen as a dark ring. Most modern guns are chambered for a $2^3/4$ inch cartridge.

ii. The Lumps: are the two steel projections below the breech end of the barrels. They engage in the action of the gun by means of the grips, or bites, cut in them and the hook of the forward lump, which hooks on to the action pin.

iii. The Flats: are the flat parts of the barrels on either side of the lumps, which meet the similar flat surfaces on the action.

iv. The Extension: is that part of the barrels which projects out from the top rib and fits into the action as an extra connection. Many guns do not have one.

v. The Extractor: is the moving part of the barrel at the breech end which, when the gun is opened, slides back and withdraws the cartridge. It may be of two kinds:

a. Ejector guns have individual extractors for each barrel, which throw out the fired cartridge.

b. Non-ejector guns have extractors in one piece for both barrels, which merely withdraw the cartridges slightly.

vi. The Bolt Loop: is the projection some inches up the underside of the barrels to which the Fore-end is fastened.

vii. The Ribs: are the steel strips between the two barrels known as the Top Rib and Bottom Rib.

Section 4. The Action

Connects the stock to the barrels and contains the mechanism for firing the cartridges, i.e. the Lock, which may be:

a. Box-Lock: most commonly made in Britain on the Anson and

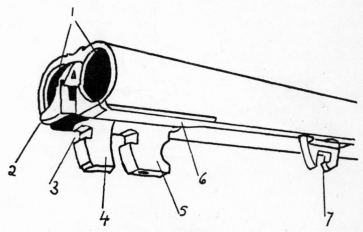

Fig. 2. The Barrels

1. Breech. 2. Extractor. 3. Bite. 4. Rear lump. 5. Hook. 6. Flat. 7. Bolt loop.

Deeley system. The simplest, most easily adjusted and best known. Fits into a solid action body.

b. Side-Lock: mounted on removable plates in the side of the action. More complex than the box-lock and more expensive to manufacture. Generally, however, preferable unless of cheap quality.

c. Dickson's Round Action: to all intents and purposes a side-lock, except that these locks are mounted on one central plate and by virtue of the design the action is particularly strong and therefore suitable for a light-weight gun.

Section 5. Parts of the Action

i.   The Bar of the Action; is that part which projects horizontally beneath the barrels when they are joined to the action.
ii. The Flats of the Action: are the flat upper portion of the bar which meet the flats of the barrels.
iii. The Strap; is the extension of the body of the action along the top of the stock and attached to it by screws. Customarily the safety catch is placed towards the rear.
iv. The Lever: is the steel arm which operates the mechanism for

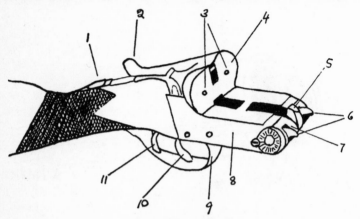

Fig. 3. The Action

1. Safety catch. 2. Lever. 3. Strikers. 4. Action face. 5. Extractor cam. 6. Cocking levers. 7. Knuckle. 8. Side plate. 9. Trigger guard. 10. Right trigger. 11. Left trigger.

locking and unlocking the barrels to the action, thus enabling the gun to be broken open. It may be:

a. A Top Lever, i.e. placed on top of the action.
b. A Side Lever, i.e. placed at one side of the action.
c. A Bottom Lever, i.e. placed under the trigger guard.

v.   The Cross-Pin: is the large screw, or in gunmaker's parlance pin, at the front end of the bar over which the barrels are hooked. In the cheaper actions this is likely to be a solid part of the action bar. In better quality guns the pin is separate and therefore removable so that the action can be tightened when loose by inserting a larger cross-pin.

vi. The Knuckle: is the rounded end of the bar on to which the corresponding concave rear portion of the fore-end fits.

vii. The Extractor Toe, or Cam: is the small hook on the front of the bar which engages with and operates the extractor mechanism.

Section 6. Attachments to the Action

i. The Trigger Plate: is screwed to the bottom of the action and projects in the same manner as the strap. It provides a framework for:

ii. The Triggers: customarily two for simplicity of manufacture. The forward trigger for the right barrel and rear for the left. A single trigger, whether selective or not, makes for greater complexity and hence greater chance of mechanical failure.

iii. The Trigger Guard: is screwed to the trigger plate and the stock. Its object is to protect the triggers from damage or from risk of being accidentally pulled. N.B.:

a. The front curve of guard must be large enough to allow for insertion of fingers of large hands.

b. The rear curve must not be too upright or almost certainly it will be responsible for bruising of the middle finger when the gun recoils. This can be cured if necessary by inserting a rubber ring on the guard.

Section 7. The Fore-end

The wooden addition beneath the barrels clipping on to the barrel-loop.

i. The concave steel fitting at the rear of the fore-end rotates on the knuckle of the action when the gun is broken and this customarily operates the cocking mechanism of the lock, also the ejector mechanism. Recesses for the cocking levers are present and tumblers for the ejectors.

ii. The fore-end is commonly held in place by a snap spring bolt, for which reason this type is known as a 'Push-Rod' fore-end. There are three common varieties:

a. The Anson, where the bolt is released by a stud beyond the apex of the fore-end.

    b. The Deeley, where the bolt is released by a metal lever set in the forward part of the fore-end.

    c. The simple 'snap' variety, which snaps into place.

iii. The Fore-end may be:

    a. Tapered, as is customary in British guns for lightness. In such guns it is usually also chequered to improve the grip.

    b. Deepened in 'beaver tail' shape, as in many U.S. guns, for convenient grip and protection against hot or freezing barrels.

    c. Variants between the above.

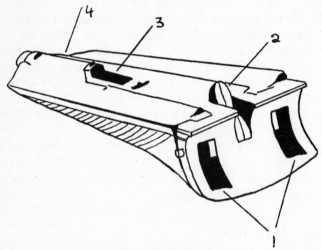

Fig. 4. The Fore-end

1. Recesses for cocking levers. 2. Ejector tumblers. 3. Slot for bolt loops. 4. Snap fastening bolt.

Section 8. *The Stock*

The wooden section of the gun attached to the action which enables the gun handler for whom it has been made to align the barrels accurately and easily on the target.

i. Usually of fully seasoned walnut because—

    a. If the wood is not fully seasoned shrinkage or swelling may result in interference with the lock mechanism, causing the gun to be unsafe.

b. Walnut is a tough and handsome hard wood, readily available.

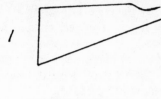

Fig. 5. Types of Stock
1. Straight hand. 2. Monte Carlo.
3. Half pistol grip. 4. Full pistol grip.

ii. The stock may be:

    a. Straight-hand: commonly used for game shooting.

    b. Half pistol grip: also used for game shooting.

    c. Full pistol grip: most commonly used for trap shooting.

    d. 'Monte Carlo': also primarily used for trap shooting.

Fig. 6. An Across-eyed Stock

    e. Across-eyed: for the man with a left master eye, shooting from his right shoulder. Cast-off (See Section 10).

    f. Variants on the above.

Section 9. The Parts of the Stock

i. **The Hand, or Grip**: is where the trigger hand grips the stock. This is usually chequered to improve the grip. The safety catch is usually positioned above it. (N.B.: This merely checks the triggers. It does NOT lock the action.)

ii. **The Comb**: rises at an angle behind the hand. The face of the stock comprises the body of the stock behind this point. Sometimes a special cheek-piece, or pad, may be added.

iii. **The Butt**: is the base of the stock and comprises:
    a. The Heel: the top of the butt.
    b. The Toe: the lower point of the butt.

Section 10. Measurement of the Stock for Fitting

Since individual build and vision vary greatly this is most important. (N.B.: The effect of a left master eye.)

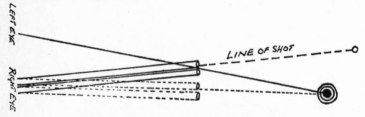

Fig. 7. The effect of a Left Master Eye

i. It is best achieved by using a Try-gun. Most other methods are liable to error, e.g. placing butt in crook of elbow and finger on trigger to test for length.

ii. Length is measured by the distances of the heel, centre and toe of the butt from the centre of the forward trigger.

iii. Bend is measured by placing a long straight rod along the rib of the barrels and protruding over the stock. The perpendicular distances from the comb and heel of the stock to this rod give the bend.

iv. Cast-off, or cast-on, is measured by placing the gun triggers upwards on a flat table so that the line of the ribs exactly coincides with a straight line drawn on the table. The distance between this straight line and a perpendicular line dropped to the table from the centre of the heel of the butt is the amount of cast. Off for right shoulder. On for left shoulder.

B. *The Various Categories of Shotgun*

Section 1. *The Double-barrelled Side by Side*

There are four principal types in this group:

i. The hammerless box-lock (ejector or non-ejector). This is probably the commonest gun in Britain. As has been shown the mechanism is inexpensive and durable.

ii. The hammerless side-lock (usually ejector, but may be non-ejector). Amongst this type are some of the best and most expensive guns made in Britain.

Fig. 8. Measurements of the Stock

1. From A to B and C to D give the bend of the stock.
2. From T to B, T to E and T to F give the length of the stock. T being the front trigger.
3. Cast-off or cast-on is the measurement of points D, B, F from the vertical line A–C through the barrels.

iii. The sliding breech, or Darne Action. Made in France, simple and strong. Noticeably light. Barrels fixed to stock. Breech is removable.

iv. Hammer, non-ejector. Foreign examples still made, but now obsolescent in this country. Advantages of simplicity, but not safe in inexperienced hands. Also distinctly slow in use.

Section 2. *The Double-barrelled Over and Under*

Usually side-lock and ejector. Favoured by trap shooters. The mechanism is more complex than is the case for side by side. The weight tends to be heavier.

Section 3. The Single Barrel

There are three principal types in this group.

i. The single barrel drop down. This may be hammer, or hammer-less, in varying qualities; ejector, or non-ejector. Usually intended as a cheap gun for rough work.
ii. Repeaters. Of two principal types differing from automatics in being manually operated:

    a. The pump gun, also known as slide action. The fore-end slides back when pulled by hand and ejects the cartridge. On being returned to position the gun is automatically re-loaded and the breech closed. The standard U.S. type carries five cartridges, but the weight distribution varies, altering the balance during firing.

    b. The bolt action. Heavy and slow to use.

iii. Automatics. Work on two basic principles:

    a. Recoil-operated. Best-known varieties probably the Browning, or Winchester. Considerable variations in types, but almost all tend to be badly balanced.

    b. Gas operated. In appearance very much like iii *a.* above.

Section 4. Magnums

This term is somewhat loosely applied to any bore of shotgun of any type which is chambered for a heavier load than is customary, i.e. with the larger chamber goes a larger load. The advantages advocated are:

i. Lightness of weight, since a smaller bore may fire a similar load to a heavier gun, but, of course, it is bound to be heavier than a normal gun of the same bore.
ii. Flexibility, since a light shot may be fired when less range is required, but the punch is there if needed.

The disadvantages undoubtedly are:

i. Heavy recoil.
ii. Squeezing of shot in smaller bore, hence stringing of the pattern.

PART 2

THE CARTRIDGE. CHOKE AND PATTERN. PROOF

A. *The Parts of the Cartridge*

Section 1. The Cartridge Case

The Cartridge Case is a closed cylinder with a flange at one end designed to fit inside the cartridge chamber of the gun and containing the charge and primer.

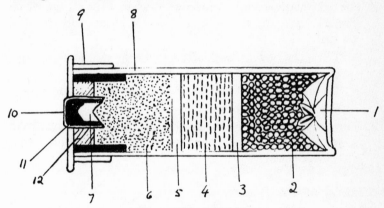

Fig. 9. The Cartridge

1. Crimp closure of case. 2. Shot charge. 3. Card wad. 4. Felt, fibre, or plastic wad. 5. Card wad. 6. Powder charge. 7. Anvil. 8. Waterproofed paper case. 9. Brass head. 10. Cap. 11. Cap compound. 12. Base wad.

i. It is generally composed of:

    a. A brass head with a non-corrosive cap, or primer, in the base, joined to:

    b. A water-resistant plastic or paper case.

ii. Its primary functions are:

    a. To act as a safe and waterproof container for the charge and cap.

    b. To seal the breech on discharge.

27

Section 2. The Cap.

The Cap is the primer which ignites the powder.

i. It is inserted in the centre of the brass head of the cartridge.

ii. It contains a substance termed the detonater compound.

iii. This is detonated by the impact of the striker pin acting against the cap and that part of the interior of the cap known as the anvil. The resulting flash ignites the powder.

iv. Modern caps are non-corrosive.

Section 3. The Load or Charge

The Load, or Charge, consists of powder to supply the propellant and wadding to confine the explosive gases behind the shot itself.

i. The old muzzle loading principle was to find the charge which suited the gun and stick to it. This had to be carefully balanced because:

    a. Too much powder was liable to blow the shot pattern apart, or cause balling of the shot, or strain the gun.

    b. Too much shot was also liable to strain the gun and to give very erratic results.

ii. The same principle of finding the charge, or cartridge load, to suit the gun still holds good today, though this point is very often overlooked.

Section 4. Modern Powder

Modern powders are fibrous or gelatinised compounds.

i. It should be realised that they are not in themselves explosive. When ignited they burn. Hence:

    a. Cartridges are perfectly safe in the pocket.

    b. Even if set afire there by some mischance, such as a lighted pipe absent-mindedly pocketed, they would probably only result in burned clothes and a bad fright.

ii. They are designed to produce the minimum fouling and smoke, but the gun should still be cleaned as soon as possible after being fired.

iii. They are designed to retain stability and consistency over a long period and a wide range of temperatures. Thus:

a. The ordinary reasonably even temperature in the house is perfectly adequate for keeping cartridges in good condition; but, even so,

b. Cartridges should not be stored in warm dry places such as airing cupboards, or in damp places.

iv. There are seven grades of Nobel powder manufactured by I.M.I. with graded characteristics, varying from fast burning, for light loads and high velocity, to slow, or progressive, for heavier loads.

Section 5. The Wadding

The Wadding is most important in sealing the bore. Felt used to be the commonest material for the purpose, but now plastics and other materials are common. Most modern wads are made from fibre and are impregnated with a special cleansing compound to remove leading left by the shot in the barrels.

i. Should the wadding fail to seal the bore the gases leaking past would be liable to blow the pattern, or cause balling of the shot.

ii. Wadding is usually inserted as follows:

a. A cardboard wad on top of the powder charge.

b. A fibre, plastic, or possibly pneumatic expanding card wad, on top of that.

c. A further cardboard wad on top of that and under the shot charge.

iii. Modern custom is to 'crimp' close the cartridge over the shot, rather than have an overshot card and turn the edge of the cartridge over on top of that. For two reasons:

a. The overshot card sometimes disrupted the pattern of the shot—invariably if slightly loose.

b. Crimp closure results in improved patterns.

Section 6. The Shot

Shot is generally 'Chilled Lead Shot' of varying sizes.

i. It is not pure lead, but an alloy of lead-arsenic-antimony. It is still made by dropping molten lead from a height inside a 'shot tower' into a tank of water. It is 'chilled' merely by falling through a current of cold air.

ii. The sizes of shot of particular note to the game shot are as follows, with their overseas approximate equivalents:

English	Canadian and U.S.A.	German, Spanish and French (Paris)	Belgian and Dutch	Swedish	Italian
BB	Air Rifle	1	OV3	9	00
1	2	3	1	7	1 or 2
3	4	4	3	5	3
4	5	5	4	—	4
5	6	6	5	3	5
6	—	—	6	2	6
7	7½	7	7	0 or 1	7
8	8	8	8	00	8

iii. The number of pellets in game charges is as follows:

Ozs. of shot				3	4	5	6	7	8
1½	...	...	...	210	255	330	405	510	675
1 7/16	...	...	...	201	244	316	388	489	646
1 3/8	...	...	...	192	234	303	371	468	618
1 5/16	...	...	...	183	223	289	354	446	590
1¼	...	...	...	175	213	275	338	425	563
1 3/16	...	...	...	166	202	261	321	404	534
1⅛	...	...	...	157	191	248	304	383	506
1 1/16	...	...	...	149	181	234	287	361	478
ONE	...	...	...	140	170	220	270	340	450
15/16	...	...	...	131	159	206	253	319	422
⅞	...	...	...	122	149	193	236	298	394
13/16	...	...	...	113	138	179	219	276	366
¾	...	...	...	105	128	165	202	255	338
11/16	...	...	...	96	117	151	186	234	310
⅝	...	...	...	87	106	138	169	212	282
9/16	...	...	...	78	96	124	152	191	254
½	...	...	...	70	85	110	135	170	225

Size of shot

Section 7. Standard Loads

The Standard Loads for smokeless powders only. The following table gives the shot charges which are used in standard factory-loaded cartridges: also included are the approximate comparative weights of the guns concerned:

Gauge	Gun chamber length in inches	Shot charge in oz.	Approximate weight of gun
12	3	$1\frac{3}{8}$	8–$8\frac{1}{2}$ lb.
12	$2\frac{3}{4}$	$1\frac{1}{4}$	$7\frac{1}{2}$–8
12	$2\frac{1}{2}$	$1\frac{3}{16}$	$6\frac{1}{2}$–7
12	$2\frac{1}{2}$	$1\frac{1}{8}$	$6\frac{1}{2}$–7
12	$2\frac{1}{2}$	$1\frac{1}{16}$	$6\frac{1}{2}$–7
12	$2\frac{1}{2}$	I	$6\frac{1}{2}$–7
12	2	$\frac{7}{8}$	$5\frac{1}{2}$
16	$2\frac{3}{4}$	$1\frac{1}{8}$	$6\frac{1}{2}$
16	$2\frac{1}{2}$	$\frac{15}{16}$	$5\frac{3}{4}$–6
20	$2\frac{3}{4}$	I	$5\frac{3}{4}$–6
20	$2\frac{1}{2}$	$\frac{13}{16}$	$5\frac{1}{2}$
28	$2\frac{1}{2}$	$\frac{9}{16}$	$4\frac{3}{4}$
·410	3	$\frac{11}{16}$	4
·410	$2\frac{1}{2}$	$\frac{7}{16}$	$3\frac{3}{4}$
·410	2	$\frac{5}{16}$	$3\frac{3}{4}$

i. The above tables explain the attraction of the magnum gun without further elaboration. BUT bear in mind:

   a. Figures can be very misleading.

   b. In practice the $2\frac{1}{2}$ inch 12 bore pointed straight is all that is required for game shooting.

ii. Now that crimp closures are general the lengths of loaded cartridges are no guide as to their contents.

   a. A nominal $2\frac{1}{2}$ in. cartridge is just over 2 in. long.

   b. A $2\frac{3}{4}$ in. cartridge may fit inside a $2\frac{1}{2}$ in. chamber, BUT may be unsafe to use since the gun was not built to withstand the pressures involved.

   c. Therefore always check the length on the box of cartridges and be careful when borrowing from a friend or using mixed cartridges in a bag.

iii. Note that Eley Maximum long range cartridges were designed for the man who did not possess a $2\frac{3}{4}$ inch 12 bore:

   a. They provide the answer for the occasional heavier load of

shot and longer range required by the owner of the normal
$2\frac{1}{2}$ inch 12 bore when wildfowling.

b. They are $2\frac{1}{2}$ inch cases containing $1\frac{3}{16}$ oz. of shot, but loaded
with a powder which does not give any abnormal pressures
and is safe to use in the $2\frac{1}{2}$ inch 12 bore gun.

B. *The Shot, Choke and the Pattern*

Section 1. *The Shot in the Barrel*

When the trigger is pulled and the striker hits the cap this causes
a flash which lights the powder. Then:

i. The powder burns and develops immediate enormous ex-
pansion of gas pressure.
ii. This pressure forces the cardboard wad forward on to the felt
wad and in turn on to the cardboard wad held back by the shot,
thus squeezing the felt wad sideways and forming a tight seal
in the chamber.
iii. The shot then travels up the barrel until concentrated by the
choke.

Section 2. *The Choke*

Choke is merely a very slight constriction towards the end of the
barrels, which has the effect of concentrating the shot as it leaves
the barrels.

i. This constriction is measured in thousandths of an inch and
each thousandth is termed one point of choke.
ii. A barrel with no choke is termed 'True cylinder'. It is sometimes possible to produce some degree of choke in such a
barrel, or increase the degree of choke in another by a process
known as recess-choking, i.e. boring a fraction out of the
barrel to leave a choke constriction. Not always possible or
satisfactory. Generally merely used for regulating existing
choke.
iii. Choke generally affects the end 2 to 3 inches of the barrel
only; thus if the barrels are shortened the choke is altered.
They are probably then true cylinder.
iv. The degree of choke and the effects of choke on the diameter
of the spread of the shot are as follows. The diameter of the

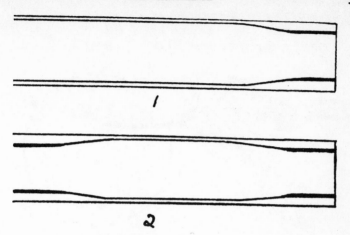

Fig. 10. Types of Choke (not to scale)

1. Ordinary choke: The constriction of choke comes at the end of the barrel.
2. Recess choke: Is formed by boring out a section of the barrel to give a similar choke constriction. Effects naturally limited.

bulk of the charge is given in inches at various ranges varying according to the degree of choke:

Degree of choke	Points of choke	10	15	20	25	30	35	40
		Range in yards:						
		Diameter of shot charge in inches						
True cylinder	None	20	26	32	38	44	51	58
Improved cylinder ...	5	15	20	26	32	38	44	51
Quarter choke ...	10	13	18	23	29	35	41	48
Half choke	20	12	16	21	26	32	38	45
Three-quarter or modified	30	10	14	18	23	29	35	42
Full choke	40	9	12	16	21	27	33	40

N.B.: The above table is for all bores, as all bores throw the same pattern circle, or spread of shot. It is merely the pattern density that varies with each bore.

v. As can be seen from the above, the effect of choke is to concentrate the shot and may thus increase effective range.

vi. It is notable that between 20 and 30 yards, probably the ranges over which most game is shot, the diameter of spread, hence the margin of error, is much larger for the open borings, rather than choke.

c

Fig. 11. Pattern of full choke at 40 yards. Pheasant missed behind and below

Fig. 12. Pattern of improved cylinder at 40 yards. Well placed above the bird

vii. The most common choke borings for game shooting are probably right barrel improved cylinder, left barrel half or three-quarter choke, but this must be a matter of choice for each individual.

viii. Screw-in variable chokes are available for single or double-barrrelled guns, varying from Improved Cylinder to Full Choke. For single barrels there are also:

a. The Collet Choke. A ring round the end of the barrel clicks over manually to alter the degree of choke, on the same principle as a drill chuck.

b. The Automatic Collet Choke. Similar variety except that the ring is automatically tightened by each shot, to increase the degree of choke.

ix. The gunsmith is not likely to be particular about the points of choke. He is more likely to concentrate on the pattern thrown by the gun and will use his discretion to obtain the best possible results.

Section 3. The Pattern

The Pattern is the spread of shot in the target area usually taken as a 30 in. circle at a distance of 40 yards for the sake of measurement. To test the pattern:

i. A 6 foot square whitewashed steel plate is required at a measured distance of 40 yards from the firing mark.

ii. The gun used should have been fired before starting or oil in the barrels may affect the result of the first shot.

iii. The apparent centre of the pattern on the plate is chosen and a 30 inch diameter circle drawn round it. The pattern is then judged on:

a. Uniformity. A good pattern is of even density without blank spaces through which the bird might fly, or balling or sticking together of clusters of pellets.

b. The number of pellets inside the circle. These should be counted and noted before obliterating with whitewash.

iv. Five shots should be fired and the average taken.

v. A blown pattern is one with the shot widely scattered, leaving large gaps through which a bird might fly. It may be caused by:

   a. A faulty loaded cartridge. Loosely packed.
   b. A faulty main wad, failing to seal the barrels.
   c. Too powerful a cartridge for the gun. Excessively high velocity cartridges are liable to cause blown patterns.

vi. A cartwheel pattern is where the pattern appears like a smoke ring with no centre and the shot concentrated on the outside. Probably due to too great a pressure as in v. *c.* above.

vii. It must be remembered that shot travels to the target in a column after leaving the barrels. This effect is known as 'stringing'.

   a. At forty yards the stringing may be as much as 8 feet.
   b. In practice it makes virtually no difference as the shot is travelling much faster than the target.
   c. Except, as noted, in the case of magnums where the stringing tends to be greatly increased owing to more shot being crammed through narrower barrels.

viii. The pattern as tested may therefore be accepted as an accurate means of learning how a gun shoots and which cartridges are best suited to it. The gunsmith will prefer this test to the purely arbitrary measurement of degree of choke. Thus:

   a. A $2\frac{1}{2}$ inch chambered 12 bore may have only 20 points of choke; but
   b. With number 6 shot and $1\frac{1}{16}$ load it may pattern as for 30 points of choke.

ix. Crimp closure of cartridges is estimated to increase the closeness of the pattern by as much as 5 or 10 per cent.

x. It is always advisable to pattern a gun with a variety of shot sizes as well as loads, since this may radically affect the pattern, especially in choke borings.

   a. Some guns surprisingly pattern better with No. 5 shot than with No. 6 shot.
   b. Some pattern well with one barrel and not with the other.

Section 4. The Effect of Choke on the Pattern

The percentage of pellets in the 30 inch circle at the following ranges varies according to the degree of choke as follows:

Range in yards:	30	35	40	45
True cylinder ...	60	49	40	33
Improved cylinder ...	72	60	50	41
Quarter choke ...	77	65	55	46
Half choke	83	71	60	50
Three-quarter choke	91	77	65	55
Full choke	100	84	70	59

With the above table, and knowing the total pellets in the charge (p. 30), it is possible to calculate the corresponding values to those, i.e.: Charge $1\frac{1}{16}$ oz. No. 5. To find the pattern at 45 yards for a half choke barrel take the total number of pellets, 234, multiplied by 50 (from table above) and divided by 100. Answer 117. N.B.: While theoretically perfect, there may be startling variations in practice.

Section 5. *The Effect of Barrel Length on Pattern*

The difference in barrel length between two guns of similar bore and degree of choke should have no effect on the pattern thrown:

i. But if the length of barrel has been altered in either case, i.e. if the barrel has been shortened, some degree of choke, if not all, must have been lost. The barrel is then probably true cylinder and no longer bears comparison with a choke barrel.

ii. In practice, pattern is to some extent affected by other factors such as the degree of chamber cone, which will affect the issue.

C. *Proof*

Section 1. *Nitro-proof*

All shotguns should be nitro-proved, i.e. they should have passed the tests of the London or Birmingham Proof House.

i. There are many old guns which are still in use but have not been nitro-proved.

ii. It is illegal to sell, give, or hire any gun unless it has been fully proved and is stamped with valid proof marks.

iii. It may be highly dangerous to use any unproved gun, especially one with Damascus steel barrels, with modern cartridges developing much higher pressures than the old black powder.

iv. The pressure induced by a standard 12 bore cartridge with

$1\frac{1}{16}$ oz. shot load is $2\frac{1}{2}$ tons per square inch at a point 1 inch from the breech.

v. When tested by the Proof House the barrels are subjected to much greater pressures than this and, if they pass, the Proof Marks are then impressed on the flats of the barrels.

vi. The Proof Marks are as shown in Section 2.

Section 2. Proof Marks.

Extracts from memoranda issued jointly by the British Proof Authorities:

i. Information as to Barrel Enlargement—Details of Proof Sizes (Memorandum on 3rd June 1959).

'Set out are the nominal bore sizes under the 1954 Rules of Proof and the corresponding nominal figures under the earlier Rules of 1925:

Bore	Rules of 1925: OLD MARKING Nominal size	Rules of 1954: PRESENT MARKING Nominal diameter
12	$\frac{12}{1}$	0·740 in.
	12	0·729 in.
	$\frac{13}{1}$	0·719 in.
	13	0·710 in.
16	$\frac{16}{1}$	0·669 in.
	16	0·662 in.
	$\frac{17}{1}$	0·655 in.
	17	0·649 in.
	18	0·637 in.
20	19	0·626 in.
	20	0·615 in.
	21	0·605 in.
	22	0·596 in.

'At proof if a plug gauge of ·729 diameter (but not one of

·740 in.) will enter the bore to a depth of 9 in., that barrel is at present marked ·729 in. and under the 1925 Rules of Proof would have been marked 12—and so on for the other bore sizes.

Rule 7 of Rules of Proof, 1954, reads as follows:

'An arm of the First Class shall be deemed to be unproved if it shall be found that the internal diameter, measured at a position 9 inches from its breech face, is 0·010 or more of an inch greater than the nominal diameter marked on the occasion of the last proof or reproof.'

ii. Black Powder Guns (Memorandum May 1960).

'A gun is proved for Black Powder only (in which case it is almost certainly over sixty years old) unless the markings on the barrel include one or other of the following marks:

UNDER 1954 RULE OF PROOF.—The proof marks at present (1981) impressed by the London and Birmingham Proof Houses are as follows.

	LONDON	BIRMINGHAM
1. PROVISIONAL PROOF		
3. DEFINITIVE PROOF FOR NITRO POWDERS on action		
on barrel		BNP
6. SPECIAL DEFINITIVE PROOF		SP
7. REPROOF		R

Additionally arms will bear markings to indicate the maximum mean pressure[1] of cartridges for which the arm has been proved together with the nominal gauge (in a diamond, as ⟨12⟩) and chamber length or nominal calibre and case length. Shotguns will also bear marks to indicate the nominal bore diameter, as found at 9 in. from the breech, shown in decimals, e.g. ·729 in.

UNDER 1925 RULES OF PROOF.—The Provisional, Special Proof and Reproof marks were similar to marks 1, 6 and 7, but the following different markings should be noted.

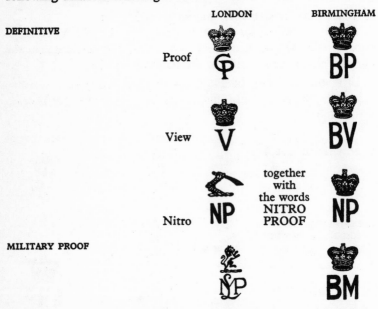

N.B. The encirclement of marks impressed under these Rules as

accompanied by the words Not English Make indicated proof of a foreign arm.

[1] *In exceptional cases maximum service loads may be marked in lieu of service pressures.*

Additionally marks were used to indicate nominal bore diameter (such as 12 or $\frac{13}{1}$), nominal gauge (in a diamond, as), chamber length and maximum shot load. In the case of rifles, marks will indicate the normal calibre and case length and the maximum service load of powder and bullet.

UNDER RULES OF PROOF PRIOR TO 1904.—The following Definitive proof marks were in use at the Birmingham Proof House from 1813 until August 1904.

BIRMINGHAM
COMPANY
PROOF

VIEW

These marks invariably indicate proof for Black Powder unless they are associated with the marking Nitro Proof in words.

Between 1887 and 1925 the following marks were used to denote special Definitive proof of barrels proved once only. They may appear on single-barrel shotguns and on certain rifled arms.

LONDON

BIRMINGHAM

'Shooters are therefore urged most strongly not to buy any gun not bearing the marks of nitro-proof and not to permit the continued use of any such gun in their possession until it has passed nitro-proof.'

Section 3. Chromium Plating

Under E.E.C. regulations new guns with the inside of the barrels chromium-plated are accepted, but as pitting is disguised old barrels chromium-plated are not acceptable to the British Proof House. They ruled that: . . .
'Barrels treated in this way must be considered to have been

potentially reduced in strength and be deemed to be unproved barrels under Section 110 of the Gun Barrel Proof Act.'

Section 4. *Foreign Proof Marks*

Under reciprocal agreements the Proof Marks on guns from the following European countries are acceptable in the U.K. and vice versa:

Austria, Belgium, Czechoslavakia, France, Federal German Republic (West Germany), German Democratic Republic (East Germany), Hungary, Italy, Spain, Yugoslavia, etc.

Metric Measurements:

From 1984 onwards all measurements may be given in metric.

BOOK 2

The Approach to Shooting

PART I

THE INITIAL STEPS

A. *The Choice of Shooting*

Section I. *Advice for the Beginner*

The complete beginner who wants to take up shooting should first obtain a shotgun certificate from the police, then:

i. Go to a reputable gunsmith and explain that he is thinking of taking up shooting and would like some lessons. It is in the gunsmith's own interests to encourage him and he will:

   a. Measure him with the try-gun.

   b. Explain the elementary rules of gun safety.

   c. Coach him in gun handling, footwork and shooting at clay pigeons.

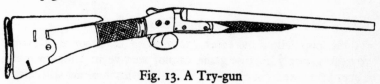

Fig. 13. A Try-gun

WRONG   RIGHT

Fig. 14. Putting the Gun together

ii. Having fired a gun and decided that he would like to go ahead and learn more, the beginner should then consider the following points carefully in the light of the ensuing sections, where they are dealt with more fully:

    a. Place, i.e. where he lives, whether in town or country, and what part of the British Isles, must influence his choice of shooting to a very considerable degree.

    b. Time, i.e. how long he is prepared or in a position to spend on his sport; whether he can spend a few hours during the the week, a day at week ends only, or merely a fortnight in the year. This must also influence his choice very considerably.

    c. Finance, i.e. how much is he prepared to spend on his sport. Shooting need not be any more expensive than golf, but it is wise to decide on a budget beforehand and choose the shooting accordingly.

Section 2. *The Geography of Game Shooting*

As the population increases the amount of shooting available decreases simply because game cannot survive in built-up areas. Yet even in the extremely crowded British Isles there are still certain clearly defined areas where certain kinds of game shooting may be expected, since the ground and conditions in such places are particularly suited to that kind of game. Roughly:

i. Grouse moors are mainly found in an area from the north of Yorkshire to the north of Scotland. There are a very few moors outside this area, in Wales and farther south, but the pick of the grouse shooting is in the north of England and Scotland.

ii. Partridges are to be found in almost every county in the British Isles, but are becoming increasingly scarce in some areas, due chiefly to modern farming methods. The centre of driven partridge shooting is East Anglia.

iii. Pheasants are also to be found in most areas of the British Isles, except in the extreme north or very hilly and exposed regions. As they are easily reared they are the mainstay of most low ground shoots.

iv. Woodcock are scarce, unpredictable and elusive, though

present in most counties in Britain and breeding in some. It is chiefly in East Anglia, the West Country and Ireland that annual migrations from the Continent make occasional woodcock shooting days possible.

v. Snipe are also to be found almost everywhere in Britain, but seldom in such quantities that they can be regarded as the mainstay of the shoot. An exception is the bogs of Ireland, where snipe days are common.

vi. Ground game, i.e. hares and rabbits, are still to be found in most parts of the British Isles, moorland, hill or low ground. There are few shoots, even since myxomatosis, where one or other is not included in the bag, though generally not shot exclusively until the end of the shooting season.

vii. Wildfowling, though strictly outside the scope of a book on game shooting, must be mentioned. It is a sport in its own right and available round the coastline almost everywhere, but many good wildfowling areas have been grossly overshot. Duck shooting, i.e. flighting duck at dusk as they come in to feed, the inland equivalent of wildfowling, may make an interesting addition to many shoots wherever there are suitable conditions for constructing a flight pond.

Section 3. *The Game Shooting Season*

The laws on shooting in Great Britain are riddled with anachronisms and not least of these are the legal seasons for game shooting, which are as follows:

Inclusive Dates

Grouse and ptarmigan, 12th August to 10th December

Snipe, 12th August to 31st January

Blackgame, 20th August to 10th December

Wildfowl (geese and ducks) and woodcock in Scotland, 1st September to 31st January

Partridges, 1st September to 1st February

Capercaillie, and woodcock in England and Wales, 1st October to 31st January

Pheasants, 1st October to 1st February

Groundgame, i.e. hares and rabbits, may be shot throughout the year, but hares may not be sold between March and July inclusive.

It should be noted:

i. There may be considerable variations in different areas and different years as to the suitability of these dates.

ii. It is accepted practice for most shooting men to set their own starting and finishing dates for the season within these limits with a view to the benefit of the shoot, i.e. so as to leave a sound breeding stock.

iii. It is not uncommon for a grouse moor or partridge shoot to be left entirely unshot in an exceptionally bad breeding year in order to improve future prospects.

iv. As a very rough overall guide, grouse may be at their best from late August to early October; partridges, October/ November; pheasants, November/December; wildfowl, December/January.

Section 4. *Auxiliary Forms of Shooting*

Other types of shooting auxiliary to game shooting with which the game shot may be concerned are:

i. Wildfowling. As already noted, a separate sport. Shooting on the foreshore, below high-water mark, continues from 1st September to 20th February.

ii. Pigeon shooting. Often involves setting out decoys and shooting from a hide. Can provide good practice for the game shot and all-year-round sport.

iii. Rabbiting, with ferret, or with dog when the holes have been blocked, can be an interesting form of out-of-season shooting and good training in quickness.

iv. Predator control. Crows, magpies and other predators of game birds should be shot for the benefit of the shoot and can provide out-of-season sport and practice.

v. Clay pigeon shooting. Can be a sport in itself, but it is always good practice for the game shot who cannot otherwise obtain opportunities.

Section 5. *The Three Forms of Game Shooting*

Broadly speaking, regardless of the principal kind of game, whether grouse or partridges, etc., there are only three main forms of game shooting, as follows:

i. Driven game shooting. The game is driven by beaters over the waiting guns.

ii. Walking-up. The guns form a line and walk forward shooting the game as it rises in front of them.

iii. Dogging. The dogs work in front of the walking guns. If the dogs work out of range they must point. The dogs find the game and point or flush it for the guns.

Section 6. *The Two Types of Shoot*

There are basically only two kinds of shoot:

i. The Keepered Shoot, where:

    a. At least one full-time keeper is maintained.

    b. Game is preserved and reared on some scale.

    c. Game is generally driven by beaters over organised parties of guns throughout the season, or the greater part of it.

    d. The dates of the shooting days are generally formally decided in advance at the start of the season.

ii. The Roughshoot, where:

    a. No full-time keeper is employed.

    b. Game is not reared artificially on any scale.

Section 7. *Methods of Obtaining Shoots and Shooting*

Regardless of the principal kind of game involved, i.e. whether grouse or partridges, etc., there are a number of ways whereby one or more of the three forms of shooting (specified in Section 5 above) on one or other of the two types of shoot may be obtained. They are as follows:

i. Ownership of the land may include the shooting rights, although in the absence of specific agreement they are vested in the occupier. Assuming this agreement, this is not necessarily the most expensive way of obtaining shooting. It is certainly the best if money is no object. The owner/occupier has every advantage.

ii. Shooting rights may be leased. The lease must be in writing and under seal. Assuming that it is for a reasonable term of years, this may be a very satisfactory arrangement.

D

iii. A shooting partnership may be formed with the owner, or lessee, of the shooting rights. As with any partnership, this may be a satisfactory or regrettable arrangement.

iv. A syndicate may be formed by a number of guns joining to share the costs of a shoot. Taking a gun, or a share in a syndicate, usually involves less than a partnership.

v. Some wildfowling/roughshooting clubs lease shoots which are run for the benefit of their members.

vi. Some hotels/estates provide shooting, which may vary from very good to very poor. It may be expensive, or it may be very good value.

Section 8. *Preliminaries to Obtaining Shooting*

The beginner usually requires to know where to start. The following pointers may be helpful:

i. The gunsmith may know of some shooting available suitable to the requirements and ability of the beginner.

ii. Sporting estate agents may be able to provide the answer to the beginner's requirements.

iii. Advertisements offering shooting in almost any of the forms covered may be found from time to time in:

    a. The Shooting Times.   *e. Shooting News.*
    b. The Field.   *f. Sporting Gun.*
    c. Country Life.   *g. Countrysport*
    d. The Shooting Life

All of which are obtainable at any newsagent on order.

Section 9. *Pointers to Costs*

Some of the methods of obtaining shooting are obviously more expensive than others, though most have been applicable to either type of shoot (i.e. keepered or roughshoot).

i. The ideal and best of both worlds is obtained by being owner/ occupier. Land values generally include sporting rights.

ii. The value of shooting leases clearly varies greatly and there is little point in trying to make any general assessments. They may sometimes be roughly checked by the local rating assessments.

iii. A shooting partnership usually involves sharing costs of keeper, rearing and beaters, etc., if any. Estimates must therefore vary with circumstances.

iv. Theoretically a syndicate should share the costs of the shoot according to the number of guns. Usually the organiser obtains his shooting free or at reduced rates. If he does his job efficiently this is probably acceptable enough to the others, but their rates are accordingly higher.

v. Hotel/estate charges may vary from over £1,000 a week (for country house atmosphere?) to ordinary hotel rates. The shooting may vary also, but it would be a mistake to imagine that the highest charges necessarily mean the best shoot.

vi. Theoretically the Game Records for previous years should always provide some idea of values. The amount of the bag, however, is seldom an accurate assessment of the enjoyment obtained from sport.

vii. Pre-1914 estimates used to be that each bird bagged cost approximately one guinea, but this must have always varied with the game, i.e. grouse, partridges or pheasants, the place, the time, the form of shooting and the type of shoot.

B. *The Choice of a Gun*

Section 1. Advice to the Beginner on Buying a Gun
As in Part I A, Section 1 above, the complete beginner should first obtain a shotgun certificate from the police and then:

i. Go to a reputable gunsmith:
  a. Explain that he wishes to buy a gun.
  b. Stipulate what he is prepared to pay.
  c. Outline the sort of shooting he is most likely to be doing.

ii. The gunsmith will advise him and probably measure him with the try-gun before offering him a choice. Then:
  a. When a suitable gun has been chosen and fitted he will probably insist on the gun being plated and some clay pigeons shot by the beginner.
  b. The beginner will thus have complete confidence in the fit of the gun and his ability to handle it.
  c. The beginner will thus have the warranty and the backing of the gunsmith's reputation behind him.

    d. This may prove a little more expensive initially, but will be a sound investment.

Section 2. *Other Methods of Buying a Gun*

The beginner will find it is always worth going to the best source available to him and buying the best he can afford of the kind of gun he requires, but guns can be bought:

i. From a gun dealer.

    a. A reputable gun dealer is the next best thing to a gunsmith. The distinction in fact is sometimes a fine one today, as few gunsmiths really make their own guns any more.

    b. The only difference is likely to be that the gun is not plated or fired, but this is a considerable one.

    c. The side-line dealer, or amateur dealer, should be avoided like the plague.

ii. From an ironmonger or sporting outfitter who also stocks guns and cartridges.

    a. Possibly all right for a new 'off-the-peg' gun, but beware of i. *c.* above.

    b. The acid test here is whether you would go to your gunsmith for a pound of nails or a beachball.

iii. Through an advertisement.

    a. The gun may be as advertised or it may not.

    b. Guns should not be bought in this fashion unless the buyer knows what he is about.

iv. In a sale: as with advertisements.

v. Through a friend. This is one way of losing a friend.

Section 3. *Desirable Qualities in a Game Gun*

The choice of a gun must ultimately always be a matter for each individual to decide for himself. Some indication of suitable choice has already been given when describing the various categories of shotgun on p. 25. The following points should also be considered:

i. The gun should always match the man as far as possible:

    a. A very small man should obviously not have a gun with

extra long barrels. They will easily pick up snow and mud
and he will find them unwieldy.

b. Conversely a very large man should not have a gun with
extra short barrels. They will tend to look and feel un-
balanced.

ii. The gun should also match the shooting, i.e.:

a. While a repeater or automatic might be perfectly suitable
on a small roughshoot, a pair of best side-lock ejectors
would be out of place. Only one would be required and
would probably prove a source of anxiety in case it should be
scratched or damaged in any way.

b. On a big driven pheasant shoot, or grouse moor, a pair of
best side-lock ejectors might be very suitable and a repeater,
or automatic, out of place. Rightly or wrongly they are
regarded in conventional sporting circles as neither entirely
sporting nor entirely safe.

iii. The gun should be as light as possible compatible with sufficient power, always remembering that a pea shooter is no use
against elephants; i.e.:

a. A ·410 gauge 3 inch magnum may be light, but lacks power
even if it may perform well in the hands of an expert shot.

b. A 12 gauge $2\frac{1}{2}$ inch side by side firing $1\frac{1}{16}$ oz. is probably
the best combination for all game shooting. Its $6\frac{1}{2}$ lb. will
be heavy enough by the end of the day.

iv. The gun should be mechanically simple and reliable. This
should be part and parcel of a good gun; but:

a. Repeaters, automatics and even over and unders to some
extent fall down on this point as well as on the matter of
excess weight above.

b. The conventional side by side is notable for both points.

v. The gun should be easy to handle. Good balance and easy
mounting are perhaps the most desirable qualities of all, but
the gun should also:

a. Open easily to enable fresh cartridges to be inserted quickly.
If it does not open widely enough it can slow reloading
considerably. Some guns open easily when not fired, but
less easily when a shot has been fired.

    b. Close with ease. Some guns which open easily require an effort to close them.

    c. N.B.: These points are further objections to repeaters and automatics. They tend to be awkward to handle, and removing cartridges to cross an obstacle can be quite a performance.

vi. The gun MUST BE SAFE. This is not just a matter of having the safety catch in a convenient position readily accessible and on Safe. It is desirable:

    a. To be able to glance easily down the barrels from time to time when out shooting to make sure that no mud or other obstruction has lodged in them.

    b. That others should be able to see clearly and at a glance beyond doubt that the gun is empty and unloaded, i.e. with the breech open as when handing the gun across an obstacle.

    c. Only the conventional gun has these qualities. Even the Darne fails on point *a.* above.

vii. The majority of points above are conclusively in favour of the conventional 12 gauge side by side hammerless gun, preferably an ejector for all forms of game shooting. But:

    a. This does not mean that the man shooting by himself on a roughshoot may still not suit himself entirely as to what sort of gun he likes.

    b. This merely means that if the beginner wishes to accept invitations to shoot game in the company of others, and hopes to have the invitations repeated, he would be advised to invest in a gun of this type.

Section 4. English or Foreign, New or Secondhand. Price

Having decided on the type of gun he requires, the beginner who wishes to buy as cheaply as possible may decide to look around before making his decision, and will promptly find that there is a bewildering range to choose from, but:

i. It has been stressed that it is worth while going to a reputable source (i.e. gunsmith or gun dealer) and buying the best he can afford, because:

    a. The reputable dealer will have the best selection of new and secondhand guns, English and foreign, available in the biggest price ranges. Comparisons can be made.

b. The reputable dealer has his reputation to consider and cannot afford to sell poor guns with his warranty.

c. Properly cared for, a good gun should not deteriorate or decrease in value and should last a lifetime.

ii. The well-made secondhand gun is likely to be better value than the modern mass-produced gun in the same price ranges.

iii. Unless reliable first-hand experience can be obtained about any foreign make of gun, it is usually preferable to buy a comparable English gun, even if secondhand.

iv. The price range from £15 to £150 covers:

a. Single barrels, some small bores, repeaters, or foreign conventional guns, and the highly dangerous.

b. With very occasional exceptions worth-while game guns are not obtained within this range.

v. The price range £150 to £500 covers:

a. Many types of new foreign conventional and some makes of English mass produced guns.

b. Quite a wide variety of secondhand game guns may be found in this price range.

vi. The price range £500 to £1,500 covers:

a. The majority of new and secondhand guns.

b. Except some best hand-made examples.

Section 5. Fitting and Plating

Should be a part of buying any gun.

i. It is well worth any extra expense in having a gun fitted, even though many people shooting all their lives have never done so and have adapted themselves instead to guns bought or inherited.

a. Secondhand guns can usually be altered quite readily.

b. If a stock is being altered the opportunity should be taken to have a gun overhauled at the same time.

ii. Any gun should also be plated.

a. The beginner can do this himself if necessary.

b. It will increase his confidence in his gun and his cartridges enormously.

c. At the same time he should take the opportunity of firing at a few clay pigeons if possible.

Section 6. *Major Repairs and Alterations*

When a gun is bought secondhand certain major alterations may be necessary.

i. Restocking. If the stock is a radically bad fit and cannot be altered successfully, restocking may be the only answer. It can be expensive. It may be cheaper to sell the gun and try again.

ii. Renewing the barrels.

There may be various reasons for this:

a. If the barrels have been shortened the degree of choke will have been altered, probably to true cylinder, and recess choking may make little difference. In such circumstances the only solution may be new barrels.

b. The barrels may be so deeply pitted that they are unsafe to use.

c. The gun may have failed nitro-proof, or the barrels may have burst due either to wear, or accident such as a blockage by mud or frozen snow.

There are two methods open:

a. Entirely new barrels can be made for the gun. This is an expensive proposition, since they must be made to match the action and the old barrels.

b. The gun may be re-sleeved, which is a much cheaper process. The old barrels are cut down to the last few inches leaving the lumps intact. Then a pair of new barrels are fitted down, i.e. like a sleeve, under the part of old barrel remaining. Such barrels must be stamped 'Sleeved' and must undergo nitro-proofing.

iii. If the action has been damaged this may mean the gun cannot be repaired, but:

a. There may be parts of the lock which require renewal or overhaul, and this is well worth checking in any case.

b. A loose action can sometimes be tightened.

Section 7. Minor Adjustments

There are several points which can be altered and adjusted once the gun is bought.

i. Pitting. Can sometimes be removed by 'lapping', i.e. boring out the barrels, but this may cause the gun to become out of proof unless care is taken.

ii. Choke. If it is felt that there is too much choke producing too tight a pattern, it is a simple matter to adjust it by removing a little of the choke and altering the barrels slightly.

iii. Tightening the pattern. Can be done by recess choking, but, as noted, where the barrels have been shortened and choke lost it cannot be replaced by this method.

iv. Weight and balance. Can both be altered by a skilled gunsmith. Sometimes to quite an astonishing degree.

v. Length of butt. Can be altered quite easily as can minor points of fitting. If a rubber pad is added it must be of the best quality and not stick to the clothes when the gun is mounted.

vi. Trigger pulls. These can and should be adjusted to suit the individual. They can be a considerable handicap if unsuitably adjusted.

    a. Hair-triggers are anathema, as well as being dangerous, and should be avoided at all costs.

    b. The commonest estimate of the correct trigger pull for a gun is somewhere around half the weight, i.e. a 7 lb. gun should have a trigger pull of $3\frac{1}{2}$ lb.

    c. The left trigger customarily has slightly more pull than the right, because the finger naturally exercises greater leverage on the right trigger since more of the joint acts on this trigger.

    d. The actual pull should be quick and crisp, not slow and dragging.

    e. Some people might like a pull of as much as 8–12 lb. For most people, however, this would be inclined to be too much, causing them to jerk off target.

vii. Some people like to have sling attachments fitted to their guns.

    a. These are fitted towards the end of the barrel on the underside and on the underside of the stock.

    b. They are all right for roughshooting or for wildfowling

where the gun may have to be carried for considerable
periods at a time and are common on the Continent.

c. They are not common in driven game shooting, since they
are seldom required there and are considered to detract
slightly from the appearance of a good gun.

d. Removable slings and fittings are obtainable, which slide
over the barrels and have a toggle attachment in the butt.

Section 8. *Basic Accessories with the Gun*

There are certain accessories which should also be purchased
when the gun is bought. These are basic essentials which are
required to maintain the gun, and although certain types of foreign
and mass produced guns are sold without them, they should (if
only mentally) be included in the price. They are:

i. A flat leather, or reinforced canvas, baize-lined fitted carrying
case is often included with the gun:

a. It is desirable to be able to take the gun to pieces, clean it
and put it away in such a case after shooting.

b. It will travel safely and conveniently in such a case without
fear of damage to the barrels or action.

ii. In the case there should also be compartments for the necessary
cleaning gear, which should also be included:

a. This should consist of a cleaning rod in two pieces. A screw
joint in the centre and strong wood or whalebone composi-
tion is desirable.

b. A variety of cleaning jags, tow or cleaning patches, oil
bottle, etc.

iii. Snap caps should also be included and there should be room
for them in the case. These are merely a pair of light metal
dummy cartridges with sprung primers, which can be used
with safety in practice without damage to the firing pin.
N.B.: The gun should never be fired without snap caps or
damage to the action or strikers may result.

Section 9. *Other Accessories to the Gun*

While buying the gun there are certain other accessories which
the beginner would be wise to buy at the same time. They are:

i. A good-sized cartridge bag.

  a. This should be of leather with a reinforced mouth which stays open. It should last a lifetime.
  b. They are made in sizes containing from 50 cartridges upwards to 150. On the whole it is worth buying the largest. There is nothing worse than running short of cartridges.
  c. It may however be advisable to buy another, or a smaller one, as two different kinds of cartridges may be required in the same day and it is not advisable to mix different kinds in the same bag. This can lead to indifferent shooting.

ii. A cartridge belt, or cartridge dispenser.

  a. A belt containing twenty-five cartridges is a useful adjunct to shooting.
  b. Do not buy one with metal open clips. They tend to become loose and cartridges can be jerked out of them when catching in obstructions, and accidentally lost.
  c. The enclosed leather loop variety are probably the best of all kinds, providing protection from the weather, though the belt should be worn under the coat in rain.
  d. The dispenser is effective enough, but is inclined to be gadgety.

iii. A leather, canvas, or P.V.C. full length gun sleeve with sling:

  a. This is extremely useful for carrying the gun between drives in a car or Land Rover.
  b. If lined with sheepskin, or kapok, it may prevent minor dents and damage, but an all-round zip is essential to dry it out after use if it has been raining and the gun gets wet.
  c. The advantage of a canvas case is that it can be rolled up into a small space and carried. It is one answer for those who do not sling swivels on their guns.

iv. Cartridge adaptors, which slip inside the chamber and enable cartridges of a smaller bore to be used, are sometimes worth having, e.g. when using a 12 bore ferreting, ·410 adaptors will prevent the rabbits being plastered.

v. If more than one gun is kept it is advisable to have a gun cabinet:

    a. This should have racks for the guns, preferably horizontally rather than vertically.

    b. It should have ample space beneath it for storage of cartridges, cleaning materials and other paraphernalia.

vi. Insurance is cheap and well worth while. There is a move to make it compulsory.

Section 10. *Care of the Gun*

With the use of non-corrosive cartridges gun cleaning has been greatly simplified, but N.B.: after shooting the gun should always be cleaned as soon as possible.

i. The use of tow forced down the barrels can damage them if too much is used and too much force applied. They can quite easily be bulged and rendered unsafe.

ii. A piece of paper (*The Times* is excellent for the purpose) 8 inches by 6 inches, rolled in a ball and thrust through the barrels, will remove all visible powder traces.

iii. Follow this by using a clean flannel patch. N.B.: Boxes of the appropriate size can be bought cheaply and are a sound investment. Made by Parker Hale. A suitable jag to hold them screws into the cleaning rod.

iv. If there are any patches of fouling still visible a brisk rub with a phosphor bronze brush will soon remove them.

v. One of the aerosol gun-oil containers is very useful for spraying the gun with a thin film, but be careful not to use too much.

vi. A pull through with the oil mop should complete the cleaning of the barrels. N.B.: It is worth having a spare cleaning rod with this mop permanently on it. Make sure it is pulled through, not pushed, or the mop will soon disintegrate. It is known as a 'Turk's Head' mop.

vii. Wipe the outside with an oily flannel rag, but have a care of the wood round the action. This should not be soaked with gun oil. It can lead to rotting of the wood or swelling interfering with the action.

viii. After a wet day make sure that the ribs are thoroughly dried by running blotting paper along them, or using a pipe cleaner for the same purpose.

ix. After a day on the mudflats or salt marshes, or when the guns have been thoroughly dirtied, hot soapy water can be used effectively on the barrels and action. Lukewarm is preferable for the stock, but don't be afraid to use a nail brush, or a tooth-brush in awkward places.

x. In very exceptional circumstances such as these it may be advisable to remove the locks (or bottom plate in the case of a box-lock), but this should only be attempted if the correct gunmaker's turnscrew to fit the lock screws is available and it is clearly understood how to do the job.

   a. When removed the parts should be dried as far as possible with the aid of pipe cleaners. They can be left to dry overnight in a warm cupboard and oiled in the morning before being replaced.
   b. It must be appreciated, however, that a gun turn screw which fits one gun may not necessarily fit another, and whereas one gun may be quite simple another may be very complex.
   c. Unless the turn screw fits exactly, burring of the screw heads will result and damage to the gun.
   d. If in any doubt whatever it is far better to wait and go to a gunsmith at the first opportunity.

xi. The gun should always be inspected for dents as it is being cleaned, and if any are discovered on no account should any attempt be made to 'shoot them out'.

   a. This merely means that a portion of the inside of the barrel has been shot away, even though the dent disappears.
   b. It is a source of potential weakness thereafter in the barrel.
   c. Take the gun to a gunsmith to have the dent 'raised' correctly.

xii. The gun should in any case be taken to the gunsmith for a complete overhaul at regular intervals. This is a sound investment. An expensive gun is worth looking after and with a little care will last indefinitely.

Further points of gun care are:

i. No gun should be left for any length of time standing upright butt down with very wet or very oily barrels, since they will merely drain straight into the action.

This can cause swelling or rotting of the wood, resulting in a weakened stock, which may ultimately crack, or else interfering with the action and possibly making the gun actively dangerous.

It might be better to stand the gun on its barrels to let it drain, or take it apart and let the action drain.

ii. Some people like to put their guns away with the lock and ejector springs eased, so that the metal is not left under tension. Some parts of the gun are bound to be left under tension even so, but be that as it may. It is done as follows:

a. With snap caps inserted the gun should be fired and then broken open.

b. While open the fore end is removed and the gun is then closed and fired again.

c. The barrels can then be removed with lock springs and ejector springs released.

d. Note however that difficulty may be experienced in putting the gun together. The ejector hammers must then be cocked by pressing them hard against a wooden edge of a bench or table. Care must be taken. Once cocked the gun should be assembled without difficulty.

iii. A baize gun case should always be left with mothballs or D.D.T. and will be found to attract damp readily, so make sure it is thoroughly dry before putting the gun away in it.

C. *The Choice of Clothing and Equipment*

Section 1. The Shooting Coat

While hard-and-fast rules cannot be laid down about shooting clothes, since they may have to be suitable for boiling hot weather on a moor in mid-August, or bleak near-arctic conditions on the same moor in November, certain points can be made. As regards the shooting coat:

i. It should always be free enough to allow plenty of movement of the arms. Anything short or tight, especially round the armholes, is liable to hamper free movement of the gun to the shoulder.

ii. There should be no padding which might prevent the gun butt being correctly mounted in the shoulder.

iii. For the same reason too much clothing should never be worn underneath the coat or difficulty may be experienced in raising the gun to the shoulder, i.e. in effect the stock will be too long.

iv. The material should merge with the surroundings, but it must be remembered that what is suitable for the moor in August may well scream against the stubbles in October or the coverts in November. A green lovat shade is probably suitable for most conditions.

v. The material should be tough enough to stand up to wear, wind and weather, but it should breathe and not cause condensation as some rubberised clothes tend to do. Tweed is probably one of the soundest materials for shooting except in the wettest conditions.

vi. Outside pockets should be roomy and toughly lined, capable of holding a number of cartridges and metal instruments such as extractors, dog whistles, etc.

vii. If a game pocket is desired it should have a detachable and washable lining, otherwise it will begin to make the coat stink like a polecat.

viii. It is advisable to have stoutly lined buttonholes and strongly sewn on buttons and a storm collar. Zips, even of the heavy gauge variety, tend to jam at awkward moments when it is least desirable.

ix. A coat of one of the tough modern oil-proofed and thornproof materials with storm cuffs and pockets, if kept well oiled and uncreased, will certainly be waterproof, but may be cumbersome and, unless well ventilated, may be like shooting in a Turkish bath. They need regular care but can be useful.

x. The ideal shooting coat should be a workmanlike job and specifically designed for shooting, not equally for fishing, or climbing, or as a 'sports jacket'. However, it should not be cluttered with useless pockets or pads on the shoulders, which serve little useful purpose and are merely intended by the tailor to impress the onlooker.

xi. Carrying a gun constantly is likely to wear a coat in the crook of the elbow and about the wearer's lower rib on the same side, but these points are seldom reinforced.

Section 2. Other Items of Clothing

Although the shooting coat is the most important single item of clothing there are several other individual points to note:

i. The head: A hat is an important item when shooting, not just for show, since when a bird is flying towards the waiting guns a white forehead stands out at once at a considerable distance. It pays to remember:

    a. A cap is all very well, but in wet weather it does not protect the back of the neck in the same way as a hat with an all-round brim, or a 'twa-snouter'.

    b. Certain types of hat, especially dark materials, stand out almost as obviously as white foreheads. The material or shade, like that of the coat, should always merge with the background as nearly as possible.

ii. The feet: The boots are amongst the most important items of shooting clothing. There is nothing worse than trying to walk far in ill-fitting boots.

    a. They must, of course, fit well and comfortably. No one can hope to shoot well if their feet are paining them.

    b. They must be tough and capable of standing up to hard wear across country and should preferably be waterproof.

    c. Wellingtons, though versatile and waterproof, are not the ideal boots for shooting. They are cold and lack support. If worn it is worth slipping a pair of light nylon socks over the stockings to prevent wear.

    d. A boot that fits reasonably closely round the ankle and has a cleated or nailed sole, allowing for a good grip and easy footwork, is desirable. An anklet or gaiter attachment helps to hold the boot in place on rough going.

iii. The legs: The ideal shooting garb for the moor is the kilt. Where there is barbed wire, however, trousers are preferable every time.

    a. Plus fours, which soak up water like a sponge in wet roots and end up with soggy rolls beneath the knees, can be a misery, but properly cut are supposed to hang away from the knees and are much favoured by gamekeepers.

    b. Shooting knickerbockers in a lovat tweed are probably as sound for general shooting purposes as anything.

    c. On a really hot moor khaki shorts might not be out of place, with puttees.

iv. The hands: In freezing cold conditions some form of gloves or protection for the hands is well worth while.

    a. If gloves are worn the trigger finger should be slit, or else removed altogether.

    b. Mittens which cover the backs of the hands and the wrist, but leave the hands free, are surprisingly effective.

Section 3. *Wet Weather Clothes*

Modern plastics and man-made scientific fibres have produced a number of light and easily packed waterproof overgarments which can be packed into a small space and produced at a moment's notice when required out shooting:

i. As with clothes to keep out the cold and the wind, wet weather clothes should not be too bulky, making it difficult to raise the gun to the shoulder. This is the fault of a great many.

ii. Especially useful for walking through wet roots are the light and easily carried stud-on leggings, which fit on easily and fastens to the belt, giving complete protection from the thigh downwards.

Section 4. *The Game Bag*

The game bag follows naturally on the clothing, as it is a part of the equipment which in some cases may in fact be worn as clothing, i.e.:

i. The American-style game bag. This fits over the clothing like a loose-fitting outer waistcoat and the game is inserted in the back. Although in some ways advantageous, as the game is easy to carry, it also has objections:

    a. It is not easy to take on or off when desired to get through fences or similar obstacles.

    b. It is not easy to put game in it oneself and requires another person to insert the game from behind.

ii. The British-style game bag is more familiar. It has a broad canvas strap to spread the weight, but even so it will tend to dig into the shoulder and unbalance the carrier for shooting.

   a. The largest size, as with cartridge bags, is the best investment in the long run.

   b. Like the game pocket, they should be cleaned out after use or they will stink disagreeably.

iii. Combination Shooting Coat/Rucksack. If shooting in a coat with two large game pockets capable of holding two hares each, a rucksack may be worn to balance them. This may either be attached to the pockets by straps built into the coat so that the weight is evenly divided over the shoulders, or the rucksack may be worn seperately as a counterweight, enabling the wearer to shoot in a balanced manner. But:

   a. An easier alternative is probably to wear an outer waistcoat over the shooting coat with large side hare pockets and a large back pocket to balance them.

   b. Anyone who is carrying six hares, each weighing some eight pounds is soon liable to lose interest in shooting.

Section 5. Other Items of Equipment

There are a number of small items it is well worth having on a shooting day which are sometimes overlooked, as follows:

i. A Shooting Stick. This is an extremely useful possession and is so often used at point-to-points and elsewhere that it is often almost forgotten that its primary purpose is for shooting. Note:

   a. It should not be too narrow. A broad seat strap makes for comfort rather than agony.

   b. It should be of metal, not wood. It may not often happen, but if the wood snaps a jagged spike might penetrate a tender part of the anatomy.

   c. The best type are all metal, adjustable for length, have a swivel seat and a broad flange at the foot to stop them sinking into the mud. A light loop for carrying is worth adding.

ii. An Extractor. This is a small piece of equipment which is usually overlooked only once. When a day has been spoiled through a hopelessly jammed cartridge it is seldom forgotten again.

a. When it is wanted it is usually wanted in a hurry and it is worth having in your pocket, but:

b. In case it is forgotten it is a good idea to attach one to your cartridge bag with a loop of cord.

iii. Game Licence. It may seem odd to include this, but it should always be carried when shooting as it may be required to be shown, and possession entitles the holder to require any person shooting to show his.

a. It runs from 1st August to 31st July inclusive. Therefore it must be taken out each year on or after 1st August.

b. If taken out on 31st July it would have to be promptly renewed the following day.

c. Before 1st November it costs £6. After 1st November it costs £4. At any time a fortnight's licence may be taken out which costs £2.

PART 2

GUN HANDLING AND GUN SAFETY

A. *Elementary Stages*

Section 1. *The Premier Rule of Gun Safety*

ALL GUNS AT ALL TIMES SHOULD BE TREATED AS IF THEY ARE LOADED, even when they are known to be empty.

ALL GUNS AT ALL TIMES SHOULD BE TREATED AS IF THEY ARE LOADED, even when they are known to be empty.

ALL GUNS AT ALL TIMES SHOULD BE TREATED AS IF THEY ARE LOADED, even when they are known to be empty.

i. This cannot be too often repeated.

ii. This is one of the major causes of all gun accidents.

iii. 'He did not know the gun was loaded' is one of the weakest excuses ever made.

iv. Always remember this and act accordingly.

Section 2. *Picking up the Gun*

When picking up the gun always try to pick it up as near as possible to the point of balance, i.e. between the grip and the fore end, thus exercising the maximum control over it, and:

i. Break the gun at once to make sure that it is empty.

ii. Make a point of glancing down the barrels at the same time.

iii. Make sure that the trigger finger is outside the trigger guard as a matter of course.

iv. Get into the habit of doing this every time you pick up a gun. One day it may prevent an accident.

Section 3. *The Secondary Rule of Gun Safety*

NO GUN MUST EVER BE POINTED DANGEROUSLY, at or near anyone; even a ricochet could kill at close quarters.

i. This is best paraphrased in the well-known words of Commander Mark Beaufoy: 'Never, never let your gun, pointed be at anyone.'

ii. The safety catch is merely a check on the triggers and should never be relied on to prevent accidental discharge.

iii. A full charge ricocheting off a concrete floor or wall at close quarters could easily kill.

iv. A close range charge of shot is lethal:

    a. Arteries, nerve ends and bones are blown apart and mangled.

    b. Anywhere in the body or head it means certain death.

    c. On any of the limbs it means certain amputation.

v. Even at a distance of 200 yards there is a chance of a pellet blinding an eye.

WRONG   RIGHT   RIGHT

Fig. 15. Carrying the Gun

Section 4. Carrying the Gun

The gun must always be carried so that it is safe. There are a variety of ways:

i. Through the crook of the arm with the barrels pointing at the ground.

    a. This is probably the most comfortable position for long walks.

  b. When carried thus between drives on a driven game day it
  is important to break the gun to show that it is empty and
  safe. In such circumstances the gun should not only be
  safe but be seen to be safe.

ii. Over the shoulder with the trigger guard upwards and the
barrels in the air.

  a. Note that care must be taken in such circumstances to
  avoid hitting the barrels against those of a companion gun
  walking alongside.

  b. The trigger guard should not be downwards. In this manner
  the gun may be pointing directly at someone behind.

WRONG   RIGHT   RIGHT
Fig. 16. Carrying at the Ready

iii. In the continental manner, held by the barrels with the butt
over the shoulder.

  a. The barrels must be broken to be entirely safe or comfortable.

  b. Unless the gun opens widely there is always a feeling of
  slight insecurity about this method.

iv. At the high port, ready to fire, the butt on the hip and barrels
pointing forward, finger over trigger guard, eyes over the
barrels looking towards likely area for game.

a. It is possible to walk forward with the gun resting on the hip in this manner, but not easy for any but the slim.

b. Do NOT be tempted to carry the gun in this fashion across the body, otherwise at each pace it points down the line at a neighbour.

v. The parasol fashion—over the arm cradled like a lady's parasol, a sheaf of lilies, or a baby—is highly dangerous. The gun is pointing, inevitably, straight at the head of the man on that side. DO NOT CARRY A GUN IN THIS WAY.

vi. At the trail is all right for commandos, but is highly dangerous when walking with a shotgun. The barrels are inevitably pointing at the legs of the man in front.

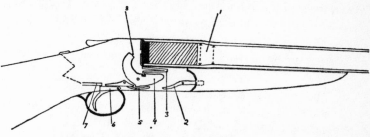

Fig. 17. A loaded Single Barrel Box-lock Gun

Principal parts: 1. Chamber cone. 2. Cocking lever. 3. Mainspring. 4. Tumbler: cocked by action of cocking lever when gun is opened; then compresses main spring. 5. The Sear Spring, which thrusts the 'nose' of the sear upwards engaging with the 'bent', or angle of the tumbler. 6. Trigger. 7. Trigger lock. Actuated by safety catch, or the action lever in an automatic safety lock. Locks the trigger blade and prevents trigger movement. 8. Striker.

Section 5. The Safety Catch

It must be always remembered that the safety catch is merely an additional security check on the triggers.

i. There are many actions which can be jarred off by a sharp knock.

ii. It is for this reason that the gun must always be carried with care and never left anywhere loaded, such as leaning against a fence, where it might fall and the barrels discharge accidentally. At the least they might be damaged.

iii. The safety catch must however ALWAYS be on safe unless the gun is about to be fired. It is a check, not a reliable safeguard.

iv. The habit should become natural of slipping off the catch with the thumb as the gun is raised to the shoulder.

v. Do NOT walk with the safety catch off when a shot is expected. This is WRONG.

vi. The majority of safety catches automatically return to safe when the gun has been broken. This is not so in some guns, notably a number of foreign ones, and can be very tiresome. It is a point to watch when buying a gun.

Section 6. *Crossing a Ditch, Fence, or Similar Obstacle*

This is the source of a number of gun accidents every year through sheer carelessness. Even when alone it should be noted:

i. The gun MUST ALWAYS BE UNLOADED.

ii. When handing the gun to someone else there are two ways of doing it:

  a. The gun may be handed over broken, to show that it is empty. If dropped, however, the gun is liable to be very seriously damaged while thus weakened.

  b. The gun may be broken first and then closed before handing over. There is less likelihood of damage to the gun in this case.

Section 7. *Putting the Gun Down*

When putting the gun down considerable care should be taken:

i. The gun MUST ALWAYS BE UNLOADED. Before putting the gun down it should always be broken first as a check.

ii. The gun should never be left leaning against a fence or wall, where it might be knocked by humans or animals and thus damaged.

iii. The gun should never be left lying where it might be trodden on or otherwise damaged. It should be carefully set down, preferably flat, in a secure place, or where the owner can keep an eye on it.

iv. If in any doubt do not put the gun down, but keep it under the arm, broken if necessary to show that it is empty.

Fig. 18. Crossing Obstacle, Safe

Fig. 19. Crossing Obstacle, Unsafe

Section 8. Loading the Gun

Loading the gun quickly and safely requires practice, and some people never realise how important it is or how much time they waste quite needlessly.

i. Opening the gun.

> *a.* After firing one or both barrels the gun should be allowed to drop to the level of the lower rib.
>
> *b.* The right hand moves forward, the forefinger against the action and the thumb against the top lever.
>
> *c.* A firm pressure between thumb and forefinger and the breech is opened however stiff the top lever may be.

ii. The gun is held fully open by the left hand on the barrels while the right hand moves to the belt, pocket or cartridge bag for more cartridges.

iii. In the case of a non-ejector the two fired cases in the breech must first be removed. This can be done very quickly with practice.

iv. When only one cartridge has been fired it is a simple matter.

v. To insert two cartridges quickly is a knack which requires practice.

> *a.* Pick two between the first and second fingers with one cartridge above the other and the lower projecting half an inch.
>
> *b.* Insert the projecting cartridge in the right barrel.
>
> *c.* Twist the wrist over and the second cartridge is automatically inserted.

vi. Most important point of all. The butt must now be raised to close the gun.

> *a.* The barrels MUST remain pointing at the ground.
>
> *b.* Should there be an accidental discharge due to some mechanical failure inside the action no possible damage can result.

vii. On no account must the common mistake be made of raising the barrels to close the gun. If this is done:

> *a.* The barrels will probably then be pointing directly at the stomach of the neighbouring gun.

b. 999 times out of 1,000 this might not matter beyond giving the gun handler a bad name and causing others to avoid him and almost certainly refusing to invite him to shoot. It is the odd time that really matters.

WRONG   RIGHT   RIGHT

Fig. 20. Loading. First Position

WRONG   RIGHT   RIGHT

Fig. 21. Loading. Second Position

viii. Another method of loading to ensure point vi. above is:

    a. When reaching for the cartridges after opening the gun slip the hand between the butt and the body.

    b. With the cartridges in the fingers as described bring the wrist and hand round the butt on the outside.

    c. The butt will then be in the crook of the elbow as the loading is effected in the manner described (v. above).

    d. The gun is then closed automatically by slipping the barrels forward slightly and raising the crook of the elbow.

PART 3

THE PRELIMINARIES TO SHOOTING

A. *Elementary Stages*

Section 1. *Preparations for Shooting*

The man who would aspire to being an all-round game shot should learn to mount and swing his gun from almost any position and to take snap shots effectively under all conditions. He must so accustom himself to handling his gun that his actions become automatic. The only way to achieve this is by PRACTICE.

i. Practise with snap caps in front of a full-length mirror daily will prove of enormous value. If the gun cannot be used otherwise such daily practice is of great assistance.

ii. The most important point is to let the muscles relax. If the muscles are taut and tense the result will be a jerky action in raising the gun and almost certainly a missed shot.

iii. The action of raising the gun should be deliberate but fluid. There should be no pause or hesitation in the swing, nor should there be long dwelling on the aim.

Section 2. *The Prepared Stance*

When the game shot is aware that game is likely to be approaching he should adopt a prepared stance in readiness.

i. The gun butt should be tucked comfortably between the right arm and the lower ribs (the instructions are of course reversed in the case of a gun fired from the left shoulder) or the hip joint, depending on the build of the individual. N.B.: It is possible to walk forward holding the gun in this fashion.

ii. The right hand should be holding the gun firmly, but not in any way tensely, round the hand or grip. The forefinger should be pointing along to action outside the trigger guard. It should NOT be round the trigger.

iii. The two points i. and ii. above should be quite enough in themselves to support the barrels, but the left hand should be loosely supporting the barrels around the fore end.

iv. The barrels themselves should be pointing upwards and the eyes should be looking over them towards wherever the game is likely to appear.

v. The feet should not be more than a foot apart, with the left foot facing roughly towards the front and the right foot roughly at angle of 45 degrees to it and slightly behind. The weight of the body should be evenly balanced.

Section 3. *The Hands and the Hold*

The manner in which the gun is held is a vitally important factor in shooting.

i. The left hand should point the barrels in the desired direction, sliding up the barrels as the gun is raised.

ii. It is a useful tip to point the left forefinger up the lower rib of the barrels at the bird.

 a. Try pointing the hand with the forefinger extended.

 b. Then reverse the knuckles and open the palm to hold the barrels.

iii. Neither the thumb nor the fingers of the left hand should be over the barrels.

 a. The thumb should lie along the left of the barrels and the fingers along the right, the barrels held between them.

 b. If the thumb or the fingers are over the barrels the effect is to deflect the eye, and hence the aim, to the opposite side.

iv. The left hand must hold the barrels level and not canted. A canted barrel means a certain miss.

v. The right hand is responsible for guiding the butt into the correct position in the shoulder, for slipping off the safety catch and for pulling the trigger.

 a. The right hand should be well under the stock.

 b. The thumb should slide the safety catch off as the gun is raised, then move round the grip clear of the top lever; otherwise it may be bruised by the recoil.

 c. The forefinger should be along the trigger guard. The top joint should only crook round the trigger as the gun comes

into the correct position in the shoulder, at the join of the
shoulder muscle and collar bone.

Section 4. *The Hold and Gun Mounting*

The hands should always co-ordinate their hold in gun mounting.
i.e. the gun should be balanced between them, each playing its
part, both complementary and opposed to the other.

i. The left hand should slide along the barrels pointing the
   muzzles on to the target until the arm is suitably extended.

Fig. 22. Raising Gun to Shoulder. Eye remains on target

  a. The arm should be straight, or nearly straight, but this is a
   matter for individual preference.

  b. The arm should NOT be wholly bent and the hand should
   be under the barrels rather than back under the fore end.

  c. This (*b.* above) is a typical beginner's hold, leading to
   extremely shaky barrels. It should be remembered that the
   fore end was originally designed to hold the gun together,
   not as a hand grip.

ii. The right hand at the grip should slide the gun up into the
    shoulder, so that the cheek is firmly against the butt, with no
    need for head movement and no disturbance of the eyes fixed
    firmly on the target.

iii. At this precise moment there should be a general tensing of the muscles and the weight of the body should move into the butt, rather than the reverse, as the trigger is pulled. At the same time the hands each grip automatically, acting to some extent as opposing forces to hold the gun rigid against the shock of recoil.

    a. There should be no jerkiness or tension, but fluid movement throughout.

    b. Any reaction away from the stock or looseness of the grip at this point will lead to bruising of the cheek, lip, finger against trigger guard, or shoulder from butt.

    c. If the action is performed correctly there should be no awareness of shot, but when practising there may be.

Section 5. The Stance and Swing

Footwork and the balance of the body are as important in shooting as in any sport. The feet are the base and the hips the pivot on which stance and swing depend.

i. Since individual builds and feet vary so greatly it is unwise and indeed almost impossible to lay down hard-and-fast rules. The following points must vary considerably with individuals.

ii. The feet should be quite close together, not much more than a foot apart, the left pointing roughly towards the target (in the case of a shot from the right shoulder). The right foot should then be roughly at an angle of 45 degrees and slightly behind the left.

iii. Weight should be evenly balanced between the feet in the prepared position, but when the bird is seen the body weight should move towards the forward leg.

iv. As the shot is fired the body weight should automatically be thrust behind the gun to absorb the recoil. The forward leg may be taking the weight, but the back leg acts as a spring absorbing the recoil.

v. When it comes to swinging round to right or left to take a shot:

    a. For the first 45 degrees each way even the average non-supple shot should be able to swing easily without moving his feet.

b. It should be possible to pivot through the full 90 degrees either way, even if it requires practice.

c. For 90 degrees or more swing to the left it may be necessary to raise the right heel.

d. Although very commonly a swing to the right is taken with the weight on the right foot and the left heel raised, this may lead to canting of the barrels.

e. For a swing to the right the weight should still remain on the left foot.

vi. Turning to take a shot behind is quite simply and naturally performed—

a. By pivoting on the inside foot of the swing;

b. And bringing the other foot and the weight round at the same instant. (Remembering to raise the barrels so that they do not point down the line of guns.)

c. A similar stance is then achieved facing the opposite direction.

vii. The movement and speed of the swing is dependent entirely on the direction and speed of flight of the bird.

a. The gun barrels should be aligned behind or below the bird and swung along the line of flight, depending on whether the shot is horizontal or vertical.

b. The body must move with the swing of the gun barrels, which must be swung through the bird.

c. On these factors the amount of swing and the moment the triggers must be pulled are also dependent.

Section 6. The Sequence of Gun Mounting

It is the co-ordination of eyes, hold, stance and swing which makes for successful shooting. From the prepared position:

i. The moment the bird is seen the eyes remain fixed on it, choosing some part, generally the tip of the beak, as the vital part it is intended to hit.

ii. The weight moves forward slightly on to the left foot as the stance is altered so that this foot points roughly towards the bird and:

a. The left hand raises the gun barrels, sliding up them to the

final gripping position, forefinger pointing (if preferred).
b. The right thumb slides off the safety catch.
c. At this stage the barrels may still be behind the bird.

iii. The eyes follow the bird over the end of the barrels as the body swings to keep them in position.

iv. The right hand raises the butt as the left arm straightens out and the barrels also begin to straighten.

v. The butt comes up to the cheek and the shoulder as the swing continues through the bird.

vi. At almost the same instant the shoulder moves into the butt firmly and the grip of both hands and the muscles of the neck tense as the finger pulls the trigger.

vii. The shoulder is firm in the butt and the weight is forward with the recoil taken by the body, but the swing continues as the results of the shot are observed.

viii. There must be no check or hesitation in the swing. The whole movement is a fluid and continuous one throughout.

Section 7. *The Commoner Reasons for Missing*

It is perhaps as well to detail the commoner faults in gun mounting, stance and swing, which lead to missing. By recognising these faults it is possible to set about curing them.

i. The following faulty left-hand holds are common.

a. Holding the gun too far back, leading to lack of control over the barrels and poor aim, generally causing missing behind, but might be anywhere.

b. Usually combined with too firm (or 'heavy') a grip too soon, making movement of the barrels, i.e. swing, slower than need be. Result missing behind.

c. Inconsistency of hold, i.e. 'tromboning' up and down the barrels, sometimes holding too far forward, sometimes too far back. Result missing also varied.

d. Canting the barrels, i.e. not holding the barrels level. A fault usually associated with wrong stance and faulty swing. Result missing behind and below.

ii. The commonest faults with the right hand are:

a. Not far enough under the grip. This can cause awkward

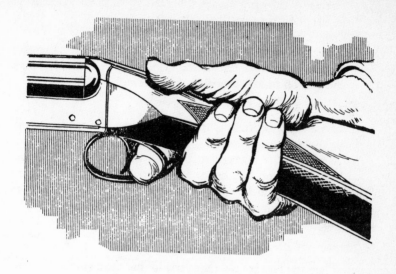

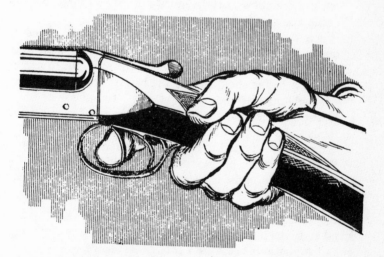

Fig. 23. Position of Right Hand on Grip

Above. Wrong. Thumb likely to be bruised against top lever, forefinger against rear of trigger guard. *Below.* Correct.

raising of the right elbow, cramped style, possibly bruising of the thumb against the top lever.

b. Infirm grip can cause bruising of the cheek.

c. Snatching at the triggers. May be due to too heavy a trigger pull or instinctive fear of the recoil. Result is likely to jerk the gun off target, probably miss behind.

iii. The results of head movement are:

a. If the head is lifted as the gun is raised the tendency will be for the barrels to rise, hence to miss over.

b. If the head is lowered to the gun the tendency is for the barrels to drop too, hence to miss below.

c. If the head flinches away from the recoil of the butt it will result inevitably in the bruising of the cheek and a miss probably low and behind.

iv. Stance can affect aim:

a. When the feet are too far apart, so that the swing either way tends to 'rainbow', i.e. the muzzle drops below the angle of swing and the shot is below.

b. When the feet are behind each other. This is bound to cramp the swing also and is likely to cause the weight to be shifted on to the wrong foot. Result, the butt fails to remain correctly in the shoulder and the barrels are liable to cant. Probably miss behind.

c. When the feet are too close together the general effect tends to be sloppy. Swing is restricted. Recoil is not absorbed by the body and the effects are much more noticeable. (This can cause bruises on the shoulder, cheek, or the second finger on the trigger guard.) The likelihood is a miss behind.

v. Rough footing can often cause a miss. When faced with a stand at driven birds in a ploughed field it is advisable to stamp out a flat platform to ensure a reasonable stance.

vi. Lack of practice. When birds rise in front of a walking gun any attempt to snapshoot off the wrong foot is likely to end in a miss. It is worth practising automatically falling into the correct stance and mounting the gun, while swinging on to an imaginary bird from a walk.

    a. It need not take more than a couple of seconds at the outside, but IT DOES NEED PRACTICE.

    b. Practice at correct gun mounting, stance and swing in front of a mirror with practice snap caps each day is the best possible thing next to regular shooting in the field.

    c. No one can expect to be any use at any sport without practice, and shooting is no exception.

vii. Lack of confidence, nervousness and jerkiness are all due to vi. above.

viii. Thinking about shooting. The process should be entirely instinctive. Practice and ability should be such that the gun is swung and the triggers pulled instinctively without any conscious thought. Once conscious thought enters into the shooting, poking almost certainly follows. Study these points by all means, when practising, but then dismiss them from the mind completely and shoot by instinct entirely.

Section 8. *Shooting Safety and Shooting Manners*

Shooting safely is more than a mere matter of observing the elementary gun safety measures already noted, although they must naturally not be overlooked. When shooting politeness is also important and consideration for others, which can often be synonymous with safety. When shooting:

i. NEVER, NEVER SWING THROUGH THE LINE, i.e. follow a bird so that the gun points momentarily down the line of guns.

    a. Imagine there is a solid pyramid between you and the guns on either side with a corner pointing at each of you.

    b. If you take it as 15 yards long on each side and about the same height this will give you an idea of the area of dead ground where you MUST NOT SHOOT.

    c. If a bird flies into that area it IS NOT SAFE TO SHOOT.

    d. It is also, incidentally, good manners to leave any such bird to your neighbour. Do NOT shoot at his birds.

    e. The same thing applies to a rabbit or hare on the ground between you and the next gun. DO NOT SHOOT.

ii. Be especially careful of firing any shots forward when you do not know whether the beaters are approaching or not.

   a. The same thing applies whenever anyone else may be in front, i.e. if walking gun, leave all birds that go forward. They will in any case provide better sport to the waiting guns.

   b. Low angle shots in any case should always be watched.

iii. Remember that shot can ricochet. Be especially careful of:

   a. Telephone or high tension cables, or fence wires. Shots can glance from them and may easily ricochet into the eyes of neighbouring guns.

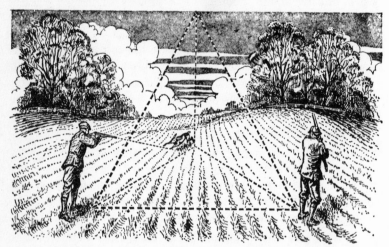

Fig. 24. Imagine there is a Solid Pyramid between you

   b. Low angle shots on water can ricochet to a surprising extent.

   c. Ricochets off hard or frozen ground are also common and in such cases it is wise to look out for dogs.

   d. Ricochets have also been known off the skulls of hares and rabbits, but are generally speaking unlikely.

   e. Ricochets off the branches of trees are not unusual and a point to watch when shooting woodcock.

iv. Whenever shooting make sure you know where the man on each side of you is placed, even if you cannot see him.

   a. In some stands at partridges or pheasants he may be round a corner as a flanking corner gun. Make sure of his position.

    b. In some grouse butts you cannot always see the next butt clearly. When making sure of your safety angles, i.e. where it is safe to shoot, it is no bad thing to mark them with a twig on each side of the butt. Some butts provide such markers and they should be welcomed, not resented as is sometimes the case. They are merely a safety factor and no reflection on individuals.

    c. Do not yourself move from where you are placed, if you are flanking gun. This may prove exceedingly dangerous. If you do have to move, make sure your neighbouring gun knows where you are or you may be shot and it would be your own fault.

v. When walking in line keep level with the rest of the line:

    a. Do not forge ahead. This is 'over-keenness', a euphemism for the shot who wants to shoot everything himself. He is a pest.

    b. Equally a pest is the man who persistently lags behind, or wanders out of line, or fails to keep his place. He is often the cause of accidents.

    c. In either case such a person is liable to get himself shot and it would be his own fault.

vi. When shooting always think ahead like a car driver looking at the road ahead.

    a. While considering whether there is likely to be game flying out of a strip of wood, notice that there is also a public footpath there, where someone might be walking.

    b. Never risk a shot where you cannot see exactly where it will go, i.e. at a bird flying down a hedge. There may be someone on the other side.

    c. Never shoot near a public road where there may be a pedestrian or cyclist passing.

    d. Remember to have a care of sheep, cattle or horses in any fields.

    e. Always have special care when dogs are about or working in front. Shots at ground game then should be watched with special care.

    f. Shots at ground game especially, and low shots at flying game, need especial care, as they usually occur when the beaters are approaching and should never then be taken in front.

PART 4

THE THEORY AND PRACTICE
OF SHOOTING

A. *Mainly Theoretical*

Section 1. The Basic Theory of Shooting

Theoretically every game bird flying within range of a game shot
carrying a suitable shotgun loaded with a suitable cartridge should
be shot if the allowances for speed, angle of flight and any drift
have been correctly estimated, the swing carried through correctly,
and the trigger pulled at the correct instant.

i. Even without examining this statement in any detail it will be
   appreciated that the personal factor involved is considerable.
ii. The Theory of Shooting, like the Theory of Economics, may
   be all very well, but:
   a. In theory a great deal can be proved by graphs and
      mathematics.
   b. In practice successful shooting depends finally on the
      individual.
iii. It is necessary to examine some of the points above in greater
   detail, since a knowledge of them can be useful to the game
   shot. But:
   a. It must be remembered that successful shooting was
      never achieved by slide rule theories.
   b. In essence the only important factor in shooting is pointing
      the gun in the right place and pulling the trigger at the right
      moment.

Section 2. The Range of a Shotgun

The range of a shotgun must vary with the bore, the degree of
choke and the cartridge, i.e. the range of any shotgun is the distance at which that gun loaded with the cartridge most suited to it
throws a reliable pattern.

i. Theoretically the range of a shotgun may be regarded as up to 50 or 60 yards.

ii. In practice shots over 40 yards should NOT be attempted unless the gun and the load are specifically designed for greater ranges, when 45 yards is still the maximum at which the average game shot should contemplate shooting.

    a. Beyond this there is too much danger of merely 'pricking' birds instead of killing them cleanly.

    b. Few game shots are competent to assess range and allowance at this distance accurately.

    c. The temptation to take long shots can soon become a vice.

iii. In practice the majority of shots are taken between the ranges of 20 and 30 yards.

    a. The appropriate tables for all appropriate ranges are included.

    b. Tables for ranges above 45 yards have not been included, since they should not concern the average game shot in practice.

    c. Tables, like slide rules, have no place in the shooting field.

Section 3. Estimating Range

Ability to estimate range accurately and at once under different conditions up to 50 yards is important for the game shot.

i. Set up various sized marks at ranges from 20 to 40 yards and compare their sizes and appearance. Shot game itself suitably set out on poles will show comparative sizes. Size can be very deceptive. Hares are often shot at too great ranges, because they are large and appear close.

ii. Get into the habit of estimating range by means of some recognised length, e.g. a cricket pitch, which is 22 yards. A distance mentally estimated as the length of two cricket pitches will then be about 40 yards. Practice will bring accuracy.

iii. Make a habit of estimating range and then pacing it out on the ground as a check, but make equally sure that your pace is a full yard, or that you know how long your normal pace is, i.e. pace out in normal strides against a measured mark. If you take 12 paces to 10 yards you will take roughly 24 to 20 and 48 to 40.

iv. Remember that distances can be deceptive in certain cases:

  a. Across water or a valley range may look farther than it really is.

  b. Looking uphill, the distance may appear more than it really is.

  c. Looking downhill, range may appear less than it really is in fact.

v. Height of a flying bird may be particularly hard to estimate if there is no landmark.

  a. Few trees are more than 60 feet high and therefore a bird flying over the tree tops is seldom more than 30 to 35 yards up.

  b. Most two-storey houses are only 30 feet to the rooftop, therefore birds flying over them are only 15 to 20 yards up at the most.

  c. Get into the habit of estimating height as well as distance and watching birds as they fly. Compare them for size when you know how high they are.

vi. Get into the habit of estimating ranges whenever you arrive at a fresh stand on a shooting day, or imagine that you are at a stand at some point in a walk.

  a. Note the distance to the edge of the pheasant covert (or it may be lamp post) in front of which you are standing. Say it is 30 yards.

  b. Do not forget that the trees themselves are about 40 feet, but if they are on a rising knoll about 20 feet high a bird may be 30 yards up or more when it is above them. Therefore it will be out of range when first seen.

vii. It is almost always the case that range is over-estimated rather than under-estimated: Try measuring in the field.

  a. The shot of 50 yards when measured is likely to be under 40.

  b. The shot of 40 is likely to be nearer 30.

  c. But there is no excuse for foolish out-of-range shots.

Section 4. The Speed of Flight

Very obviously the speed of a flying bird must vary with the bird and the conditions at the time of flight. Many experiments have been made to try to determine the speed of flight of various birds:

i. Pigeons have been timed at over 60 m.p.h. Given a strong following wind this does not seem unreasonable.

ii. 40 m.p.h. is reckoned as the average speed of a pheasant in flight, but again the question of cross-wind or following wind must be borne in mind.

iii. In general the larger the bird the faster it will fly, or so it would seem. Anyone who has seen blackgame outflying grouse on a moor will appreciate this point.

iv. No tables giving the speed of flight of game can hope to be accurate under varying conditions.

v. It is doubtful in the extreme if they are even accurate over the correct averages in the first place.

Section 5. *Shot Sizes Required for Game*

Major Burrard in his well-known work *The Shotgun* painstakingly worked out the suitable shot sizes required for various game on the basis of the size of the vulnerable area of each bird and the number of pellets required to make a clean kill by a study of the known patterns thrown. His results were as follows:

Game	Shot size	Minimum pattern in 30 in. circle
Goose, Capercaillie, Blackcock ...	3	70
Hare	4	100
Duck	4	100
Teal	5	110
Rabbit	5	120
Pigeon	6	130
Pheasant	6	120
Grouse	6	130
Partridge	6	130
Woodcock	7	150
Snipe	8	270

Nowadays No. 6 shot is probably adequate for all game when shot within normal range throughout the year. For game shooting, excluding hares, No. 7 shot is adequate for most purposes. Loads should always be suited to the gun.

Section 6. The Table of Forward Allowance

In the *Shooter's Year Book* (an excellent publication by I.C.I.) is included the following Table of Allowances, for aiming in front of birds crossing at 40 miles per hour, using Standard Game Cartridges.

Range in yards:	20		30		35		40		45	
Size of shot:	ft.	in.	ft.	in.	ft.	in.	ft.	in.	ft.	in.
3	3	4	5	4	6	6	7	10	9	0
4	3	4	5	5	6	6	7	10	9	1
5	3	4	5	5	6	7	7	11	9	4
6	3	4	5	6	6	8	8	0	9	6
7	3	4	5	6	6	10	1	9	9	8

Approximate allowance in feet

All sizes ...	$3\frac{1}{4}$	$5\frac{1}{2}$	$6\frac{3}{4}$	8	$9\frac{1}{2}$

Section 7. The Theory of Forward Allowance at a Crossing Shot

With the aid of the foregoing tables it is theoretically a simple matter of mathematics to calculate the required forward allowance for any bird crossing in front of the game shot. The application of the tables is as follows:

i. The bird is identified correctly and a cartridge loaded with the correct size of shot is chosen. (N.B.: Only one cartridge is required. It is a theoretical cartridge anyway.)

ii. While the gun is theoretically loaded the range of the bird should be correctly estimated. The distance to be calculated from the muzzle. of the gun.

iii. The exact speed of the bird must also be correctly estimated so that the necessary calculations can be made from the tables.

iv. The gun must then be mounted and theoretically swung to allow the correct distance as calculated in the table under Section 6.

v. The theoretical bird is then theoretically bound to be cleanly shot.

Unfortunately this theory does not take into account:

i. The bird crossing at an angle, when the allowance must be halved or quartered.

ii. The bird which has a curl in its flight and the wind behind it, when the theory is simply blown wide open.

iii. The personal element which is all-important in shooting:

    a. Distance, or speed, judged by one man will be bound to differ radically from the next.

    b. The time lag between swing, muzzle on target, and trigger pull will vary with each game shot.

    c. It would be just as sensible to try to teach a batsman by calculating the speeds and angles of the cricket ball.

N.B.: It is to be hoped that this proves conclusively to anyone not previously convinced of the fact that tables of mathematical calculations, graphs and theoretical estimates of this nature are best forgotten and ignored in practice.

i. They not only mean nothing.

ii. They are actively misleading.

iii. Pay no attention to them.

Section 8. *The Individual Time-lag*

The time which elapses between the eye and the gun focusing on the bird and the message being passed from the brain to the trigger finger varies immensely with individuals.

i. With this time lag also vary the ideas each individual has as regards:

    a. The range at which the bird is flying.

    b. The speed at which the bird is flying.

    d. The allowance, if any, he should make for the above.

ii. From this it follows that each individual must learn by experience and practice only.

iii. In general once he starts thinking about any of the above he is almost certain to miss.

B. *Mainly Practical*

Section 1. *The Going Away Shot*

The shot at a bird flying directly away from the gun is one of the commonest encountered when walking-up, or dogging. It should be an easy shot, but is all too often missed. However not all going away shots are similar. There is:

i. The Going Away Shot Low Down.

  a. The bird which rises at one's feet and streaks away low is a common one on the moors.

  b. The first action is to take up the correct stance coolly and deliberately, without excitement or hurry. Feet correctly placed, eye on the bird over the muzzle of the gun as described.

Fig. 25. The Going Away Shot Low Down. Forefinger pointing down barrels. Shoot above the bird

  c. It is most important to restrain the impulse to shoot at once. Let the bird fly 15 or 20 yards at least.

  d. The second action, when the bird is at a reasonable range, is to mount the gun, leaning well forward from the hips. Let the muzzle pass through the bird blotting it out as the trigger is pulled, i.e. shoot above the bird.

N.B.: Likely reasons for missing, or wounding behind, have mostly already been covered on p. 82, but note:

  a. Many more such birds are missed through being shot at too soon than being shot at too late. Too hurried a shot before the bird has reached a reasonable range is likely to result in a miss or blowing the bird to pieces. The shot pattern simply has not had time to expand.

b. Failure to blot the bird out with the barrels, i.e. keeping it in view over the barrels and aiming directly at it inevitably leads to wounding behind.

c. Excitement, lack of confidence, jerkiness, hurry, etc., as noted all lead to missing.

Fig. 26. The Going Away Shot Low Down. *Left*, wrong. *Right*, correct

ii. The Going Away Shot Rising Rapidly.

a. The classic example of this is the springing teal, or the rocketing pheasant close at hand.

b. Again the first action is to take up the correct stance as above.

c. Again it is important to let the bird fly, and not be panicked into shooting too soon. In this case it may level out, or slow down its rate of rise.

d. Again the second action, when the bird is at a reasonable range, is to mount the gun, swing upwards through the rising bird and pull the trigger on passing the beak.

N.B.: Reasons for missing or wounding behind are:

  a. Failure to swing through cleanly, or checking the swing.

  b. Taking the shot too soon or too hurriedly.

  c. In the case of a bird at 30 to 40 yards range it is important to swing well through, or it will be missed below.

  d. Any of the reasons already noted.

iii. The Going Away Shot High.

  a. Probably most frequently encountered as a second shot taken behind at driven game.

Fig. 27. The Going Away Shot High. Left hand gun, barrels canted, bird winged. Right hand gun, correct

  b. The first action is to take the correct stance with the eye on the bird over the muzzles of the gun. N.B.: The muzzles will be moving forward and down.

  c. There is usually no question of allowing this bird to fly to a suitable range, but the shot should not be hurried.

  d. The gun should be mounted, with the muzzles moving forward and down with the bird still visible above the barrels as the trigger is pulled.

N.B.: Reasons for missing or wounding behind.

  a. Blotting the bird out, i.e. shooting behind. This is one of the few shots where the bird is seen above the barrels as the trigger is pulled.

b. Too hurried a shot, because of fear that it will be out of range and swinging the barrels up; not with the flight of the bird, i.e. shooting behind.

c. Swinging through from behind may lead to poking, or deliberate aiming as the bird is brought into the line of vision again. Other reasons as above.

Fig. 28. The Going Away Shot, downhill

iv. **The Going Away Shot Downhill.**

a. This is not an uncommon shot on a grouse moor, especially dogging, or on the high tops at ptarmigan.

b. In effect it is precisely the same shot as the one above, No. iii., if the birds are flying steeply down the hill, having passed over, or in front of the gun; it is necessary to shoot below them, i.e. the bird is seen above the barrels at the instant the trigger is pulled and flies into the shot pattern.

c. Remember that range may be deceptive in such conditions.

v. **The Going Away Shot Across a Valley.**

a. This must not be confused with No. iv. above.

    b. In practice it will usually be seen to be quite a different shot.

    c. It should be treated as a going away shot low, No. i.

    d. Remember that range may be deceptive in such conditions.

vi. The Going Away Shot at Eye Level.

    a. This is a shot which should always be treated with the greatest care as to background, i.e. the presence of any beaters or others, or animals.

Fig. 29. The Going Away Shot, across a valley

    b. The gun should be mounted, as above, and the bird simply blotted out as the trigger is pulled.

N.B.: Reasons for missing, as with all going away shots, but perhaps notably with this particular one:

    a. A tendency to 'aim' down the barrels, resulting in a poking action and a miss.

    b. A tendency to take the cheek from the butt too soon, resulting in head movement and a miss.

vii. The Going Away Shot at an Angle.

    a. If the bird's head can be seen on one side of its body it must be appreciated that it is not in fact flying straight away, but at an angle towards the side the head is visible.

b. In a strong cross wind, or when one of an exploded covey has swung back at the sight of the guns, such a bird may have a very considerable and extremely deceptive curl in its flight.

c. In the case of *a.* above the bird should be treated as any other going away bird, but let the muzzles pass through the head as the aiming mark; the swing through being on the line of flight to right or left.

Fig. 30. Going Away Ground Shot

d. In the case of the very obviously curling bird it may be as well to regard the inside wing of the curl as the aiming mark and swing through that as the bird will be drifting decidedly to right or left. Swing on the line of the curl.

viii. The Going Away Ground Shot.

a. As with the bird flying away low, the barrels must pass through the game at the instant the triggers are pulled.

b. Don't be hypnotised by the white scut and hindquarters. Swing through them and blot out the ears. Use the head as the aiming mark and swing the barrels through it.

c. In the case of any ground game rising near one's feet it is

particularly easy to shoot too soon before they are at a
suitable range. See remarks above.

d. In the case of hares, however, remember that they often
look nearer than they really are because of their size. Do
NOT be tempted to take shots at them at long range which
may only wound, particularly if loaded with No. 6 shot
or above.

Fig. 31. Hare killed at 20 yards. Improved cylinder pattern. Correctly
placed

Section 2. *The Approaching Shot*

The shot at an approaching bird is the commonest encountered
on a driven bird day. As with the going away birds, there are a
variety of shots possible.

i. The Approaching Low Shot (At Eye Level).

a. This is a shot which must be taken with considerable care
to ensure that it is safe to fire. Check for beaters and dogs
within range first.

b. If in any doubt do NOT shoot. Take it behind instead.

c. The first action is to line the bird up over the muzzle of the gun in the normal way.

d. When it is estimated that the bird is 45 yards away the gun should be mounted and muzzle raised through the bird's beak. As the bird is blotted out the trigger is pulled.

N.B.: Reasons for missing are:

a. Raising the muzzles too high and shooting over the bird.

b. One danger with all approaching shots is leaving it too late and allowing the bird too close so that pattern spread is reduced and the bird missed. If the bird is hit it is smashed.

Fig. 32. Approaching Shot (eye level)

c. A tendency with most approaching shots is to lean backwards and take the cheek from the stock as the bird approaches, resulting in a miss. Lean well into these birds with the weight well forward.

d. Other reasons for missing have already been noted above.

ii. The Approaching Low Shot (below the gun).

a. This is a shot quite often encountered on grouse moors and presents certain problems.

b. If it is approaching up a slope it is really a rising shot and should be treated as an eye-level bird as i. above.

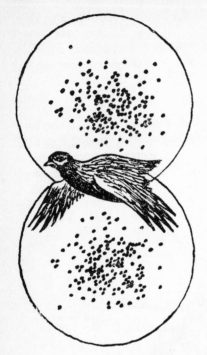

Fig. 33. Grouse missed at 20 yards with full choke above and below

Fig. 34. The Approaching Low Shot (below the gun)

c. If it is likely to remain below the gun skimming the ground, or is crossing a valley below the gun, it should be treated as a shot at ground game. That is:

d. The first action is to line up the bird over the muzzle of the gun.

e. It will be found that the barrels are being lowered to keep the bird in view above the muzzle.

f. As the gun is mounted the trigger is pulled with the bird still in view with the beak as the aiming point, i.e. the swing is forward and down, weight into the shot.

N.B.: Reasons for missing are:

a. Blotting the bird out with the muzzle, hence missing behind.

b. Leaving it too late, leaning backwards and taking the cheek off the stock, as above, or reasons as above.

iii. The Approaching Shot at Ground Game.

a. This is a shot which should always be treated with great care, since there are generally beaters or dogs close when ground game breaks forward. If there are do NOT shoot.

b. It should be treated like a shot at an approaching bird below the level of the gun. See above.

c. Do NOT shoot at a hare until you can see the eyes clearly, just above the muzzle of the gun.

d. The reasons for missing are as above.

iv. The Approaching High Shot.

a. This is a common bird in any form of driven shooting, though particularly associated with high pheasants.

b. In practice the high partridge on downland, or grouse on moor, or even duck on a marsh, may be far more difficult since without trees at hand it is far harder to estimate range and height, or speed.

c. It will usually be seen from a considerable distance, but the tendency to raise the gun too soon must be firmly resisted.

d. It should be lined up over the barrels in the normal way.

e. Only when it is estimated to be within 45 yards range should the gun be mounted and swung through from the tail past the beak, blotting the bird out at the moment of trigger pull.

N.B.: The reasons for missing are:

    a. The tendency to raise the gun too soon is very hard to withstand and the result inevitably is a tendency to poke or aim the gun which inevitably results in missing behind.

    b. Weight on the wrong foot, or leaning backwards, will tend to check the swing and the other common faults will also cause a miss behind.

Section 3. The Crossing Shot

In practice the crossing shot is amongst the simplest of all shots if properly executed. The theory of forward allowance has already been examined and, it is to be hoped, dismissed. Some allowance may be necessary, but it is generally inherent in the correctly swung gun, otherwise it is a matter for each individual to decide for himself as follows:

i. The gun should be mounted and swung as described in the section on gun mounting.

    a. The muzzles following the bird's flight from right to left or left to right should be swung freely and easily through the line of the bird's flight and over its back so that the barrels obscure its head.

    b. Without any cessation of swing the trigger should be pulled at the moment the head is reached.

    c. The barrels continue to swing, cheek firmly against the stock.

ii. For most normal crossing shots this should be quite sufficient.

    a. Especially bearing in mind that most crossing shots are at a slight angle, which decreases the amount of lead required.

    b. In any event, for crossing shots within the 20–25 yard ranges this is almost certainly adequate.

    c. If the swing is in no way checked the average time lag between mind and trigger pull will make up the natural forward allowance required, without any need for mental mathematics.

Fig. 35. The Barrels following the bird as the gun is raised for a
Crossing Shot

Fig. 36. Duck missed behind at 40 yards improved cylinder. Full
choke, second barrel, well up and above. Correctly placed

Fig. 37. Through and Above

iii. It may however be found that on the longer crossing shots the shot is falling behind the target.

   a. When firing at a crossing covey aiming at the front bird at 35 yards, the second or even second and third may be seen to fall instead.

   b. This is the effect of the stringing of the shot (a column some 8 feet long approximately at 40 yards) and failure to swing through far enough or fast enough.

   c. This tendency may be exceptionally plain on the left-to-right swing, when there is anyway a tendency to rainbow, i.e. drop the barrels, or if the weight is on the wrong foot, when the barrels may be canted, resulting in shooting low.

iv. The answer then is to increase the swing deliberately through and above the head of the bird, consciously swinging clear beyond before pulling the trigger.

   a. This involves speeding the swing, which is probably all that is required, since the tendency is to swing too slowly at the birds at longer ranges.

   b. The amount of this forward swing required is likely to vary with each individual, since it depends entirely on the personal time lag between eye and trigger.

   c. Each shot must learn his own measurements of the distance required. What may appear a matter of yards to one may seem feet or even inches to another. Yet another may never be conscious of making any allowance.

   d. Although gravity has little effect on shot it is as well to aim above long crossing shots as well as forward, because this gives the shot stringing full chance to take effect. It also ensures the barrels being kept up and makes a hit in the head more probable.

v. For crossing shots at ground game this is important. It is also important to remember with such shots to make sure there is no chance of a dangerous ricochet. The gun should swing right through above the scut and hindquarters and above the full length of the body, the trigger being pulled as the head is passed.

vi. Reasons for missing are almost certainly amongst those noted; particularly failure to swing through sufficiently far, fast or

Fig. 38. Correct Swing Through and Above

Fig. 39. Swinging Across and Dropping the Barrels. Below and Behind

high enough, canting the barrels or rainbowing, i.e. missing behind and below. Otherwise any of the reasons liable to cause missing as stated already.

Section 4. *The Overhead Shot*

This is a shot which looks extremely good when well and cleanly performed, but once learned is no more difficult than most other shots:

i. The approaching bird should be lined up over the muzzle in the normal way.

    a. The barrels must not be raised too soon, as is the case for an approaching high bird.

    b. Otherwise the result will be, as in that case, a tendency to poke and miss behind.

ii. As it approaches about 10 o'clock the gun should be swung through, weight well on to the left foot, right leg slightly bent, thrusting the barrels through the bird.

    a. The gun must be swung clean through tail and beak and the bird blotted out.

    b. Due allowance may be given for a high bird, which can be complicated by not being able to see the bird.

    c. However the rate of swing will tend to compensate for this and the trigger pull as the barrel swings through the beak will probably be correct.

    d. Otherwise the individual will have to learn his own allowance as in the matter of the crossing shot.

iii. In practice the majority of overhead shots are probably between 20 and 25 yards up and should be easily enough downed by the average shot if his stance and swing are correct.

iv. The true high overhead bird 40 yards up looks, and is, an extremely high bird indeed.

    a. Remember that speed of swing is all-important and also:

    b. The swing must not be checked, but continued right back after the trigger pull.

    c. If the weight is on the left leg with the right heel slightly raised, as described, it is possible to swing cleanly right back, but practice is essential.

RIGHT   WRONG

Fig. 40. Overhead Shot. *Left*, Dead bird. *Right*, Wounded bird

   d. If the weight is on the right foot and the gun is in the right shoulder the swing will be checked and can then only be continued back by a conscious jerk from the hips. This is a common fault.

v. Reasons for missing are as given above, but almost more than any other shot this one is missed through lack of confidence. Confidence is all-important always in shooting, and in these shots where they can be seen from a distance even more so than usual. In particular, reasons otherwise are:

   a. Raising the gun too soon, i.e. poking, missing behind.
   b. Checking swing, i.e. missing behind.
   c. Failure to swing determinedly through the bird, before trigger pull. This is liable to cause pricked or wounded birds. As with a rising bird do NOT be hypnotised by a pheasant's long tail. Swing clean through beyond the beak.

Section 5. *The Snap Shot*

A bird, or ground game, crossing a ride, or a gap, where it is safe to shoot often presents a problem, since there is apparently no room to swing and the shot must then be 'snapped'.

i. In practice what happens here if the shot is correctly executed is that the gun is mounted and swung at speed and the trigger pulled in such rapid sequence that it all appears to be one movement, and even the shot himself fails to appreciate what he has done since it has been entirely instinctive.

ii. Any attempt to aim will lead inevitably to poking and clean missing.

iii. Snap shooting at woodcock, or snipe, is often the only way to down them and can appear, and is, excellent shooting correctly performed, but:

   a. It is nothing more than the normal shot speeded up.
   b. In no circumstances should snap shooting be allowed to become dangerous.
   c. It is instinctive shooting, but it should be controlled.

iv. Reasons for missing a snap shot are:

   a. Any delay or check in gun mounting.
   b. Conscious thought or aim.
   c. Any of the other reasons for missing a normal shot.

Section 6. The Sitting Shot

Though technically not a 'sporting' shot there are occasions when it is not only desirable but essential that a sitting shot should be taken, i.e.:

i. When a wounded bird is seen to perch on a branch, or wounded ground game to halt in front of the gun, it is most desirable that a shot should be fired at once with the object of killing them cleanly.
ii. Surprisingly this is a shot which can be quite easily missed and there are even some shots who prefer not to take it rather than fail to hit it.
iii. In practice there should be no difficulty about it:
   a. The first action is to line up the bird, or ground game, over the muzzle of the gun in the normal way.
   b. The second action is to mount the gun with the target still visible over the barrels as if it was desired to skewer it, i.e. the normal swing should be concentrated in the forward movement of the gun mounting and the trigger pull must be instantaneous with the shoulder moving into the butt. N.B.: The target should NOT be blotted out.
iv. Reasons for missing are a tendency to blot the target out and thus fire over it, also:
   a. Cartwheeling of pattern. (The usual excuse.)
   b. The feeling that it is too easy, or that you are going to miss, i.e. lack of confidence, or carelessness.
   c. Deliberate aiming or removing cheek from the butt, poking, gun movement and the usual reasons for missing given above.

Section 7. The Right and Left

When a shot is taken with the right barrel and the gun is then swung on to a second target and the left barrel is also fired and both shots are cleanly killed, this is known as a Right and Left.

i. In practice it may well be the case that the left barrel was fired first and the right second. In this instance it might be technically correct to call it a left and right, but the term right and left is commonly used.

ii. If the butt is removed from the shoulder between the firing of the shots, however briefly, they do not qualify strictly as a right and left.

iii. No second barrel should ever be attempted unless it is certain that the first barrel has been successful.

iv. Reasons for missing an often otherwise simple right and left are:

   a. Removing the cheek from the stock to observe the first shot; keeping the eye on it too long.

Fig. 41. *Right*, at Low Bird, and *left*, at High Bird

   b. Checking the swing on the second bird, rainbowing, canting the barrels, etc.

   c. Failure to make a decisive choice of birds and hence firing into the 'brown', i.e. the mass, known as 'browning' a covey and a heinous offence, since several are likely to go off pricked by a pellet to die later.

   d. Excitement, hurried swing, lack of confidence and any of the customary reasons.

Section 8. *The Shot in Front and Behind*

Although not technically a right and left, since the gun must be lowered from the shoulder when turning, a shot well taken in front and another successful behind may be equally deserving of praise.

i. The gun must NEVER be swung through the line of guns. This cannot be repeated too often.

ii. If it is impossible to take two birds in front, one after another, the first should be shot cleanly: Then

   a. The butt must be lowered from the shoulder and the barrels kept upright. Do NOT try to turn with the butt in the shoulder. This will entail swinging through the line and in any case merely leads to missing.

   b. The shot must pivot on the inside leg, turning as far as possible with the bird.

   c. This may be impossible with a bird directly overhead, but is feasible with a bird to the side.

   d. Taking the correct foot position, the gun should then be raised and swung through from behind the bird if contact has been lost; the trigger should be pulled with the bird visible above the barrels and the barrels swinging downwards through the line of flight.

   e. If the bird flies past low, or in the case of ground game, contact may be maintained visually and the eyes and fore-finger should remain in contact with the target even though the barrels are raised upright. Thus when the feet are correctly placed it is merely a question of continuing the swing in the normal manner (i.e. upwards and over the target).

iii. Reasons for missing the shot behind are usually bad footwork, otherwise any of the reasons noted.

Section 9. *Shooting with a Pair of Guns*

Anyone can shoot with a loader and a pair of guns, but shooting more and better with a loader than would be possible with one gun alone is the hall-mark of a good shot.

i. It is desirable that the guns should be a matched pair made for the man himself in the first place, but anyway:

   a. They should match in trigger pulls. This will be much more noticeable with a pair of matched guns than otherwise.

b. They should also match in barrel borings, so that there will be no difference between either in the pattern thrown by the barrels.

c. The weight and handling qualities of the two guns and all other details should of course be identical.

d. In practice this matching can usually be achieved by a good gunsmith even when a pair of guns were not originally made as a pair.

e. At the very worst they should be as nearly matched in the above respects as possible. If there are any great differences it would probably be better to shoot with only one gun.

ii. Both the loader and the shot must be practised in the drill of shooting with a pair of guns, but also:

a. The shot should be a more than competent performer at driven game with one gun before he starts to shoot with two.

b. The loader should know not only how to handle guns and load competently, but a good deal about game birds and shooting. He can then be of considerable assistance to the shot, but will probably be too busy to mark the fall of the birds. This should not be expected of him.

iii. The customary drill for loading is as follows:

a. On firing one or both barrels the shot slips on the safety catch with his thumb, bringing the gun back, held muzzles upright by his right hand round the grip about the level of his elbow.

b. While keeping his eyes front on the next bird at the same moment his left hand reaches back, palm outstretched to the left of the gun.

c. The loader standing behind him and to his right grasps the empty gun at the base of the fore end, at the same instant thrusting the upright fore end of the loaded gun into his grasp (safety catch on).

d. The shot swings the barrels directly on to his next target, while the loader bends sideways out of his possible line of fire, and breaking the gun swiftly and safely re-loads.

e. As the shot fires the loader returns to the upright position preparatory to changing guns once more.

Fig. 42. Shooting with a Pair of Guns

C. *Points on the Shooting Field*

Section 1. *The Invitation to the Shoot*

There are a number of points concerning this which may be overlooked:

i. It is important, as well as a matter of politeness, to answer an invitation to shoot as soon as possible:

   a. So that the host will not be kept waiting until the last minute before he knows whether he has sufficient guns or not.

   b. Because those who do not answer in time are not likely to be asked a second time.

ii. When answering any queries should also be checked. It is important to know what sort of day it is going to be, i.e.:

   a. Walking-up, driven, or dogging, mainly in roots (possibly soaking wet), or a combination of walking and driving.

   b. Whether one gun will do or a pair will be required.

iii. It is desirable to know whether a dog should be taken if you have one, as every shooting man should.

   a. But regard must be had as to the state of the dog's training.

   b. It is never a good move to inflict an untrained, unruly, quarrelsome dog on someone else, however good a friend.

iv. If you have a keeper, or loader, you should enquire whether he will be welcome before bringing him.

   a. He almost certainly will be, but it is a matter of politeness to ask.

   b. Like your dog, he should be experienced and neither unruly or quarrelsome. You will be judged by both.

Section 2. *On Arrival*

It is extremely important to make a point of always arriving at least a quarter of an hour before the time specified in a shooting invitation. This is not just excessive politeness:

i. Inevitably there will be some points of dress to attend to:

   a. It is not usually comfortable to drive in shooting boots and they will usually have to be put on.

  b. The gun will usually have to be assembled and it is just as well to give it a last-minute check.

  c. The cartridge bag may need filling, or the cartridge belt.

  d. Shooting coat, hat, possibly game bag, if it is required; loader and dog, if present, must be prepared.

ii. The host must of course be greeted promptly, but:

  a. There are the other guns to meet and be introduced to if you do not already know them.

  b. There is the question of a number to be drawn if these are not allotted by the host arbitrarily, as is often the case.

  c. On your number depends your place in the line at each stand, or when walking up, and as it is customary to move up two after each stand it is important to remember it.

  d. There are instructions to be received on the etiquette of the day, i.e. whether hens are being shot, or blackgame, and whether it is encouraged to shoot vermin. (There may be a sweepstake on the number of head shot.)

iii. i and ii above take time and it is doubtful if the shot will have much time to spare. In any case:

  a. He should find out which are his neighbouring guns on either side.

  b. He should make a point of breaking his gun and carrying it empty under his right arm right from the start.

  c. At the same time he should avoid any damage to his barrels amid the to-ing and fro-ing that is bound to be going on.

  d. He should make a point of being there and ready to start at the appointed time.

Section 3. *At the Stand*

At the risk of seeming uncommunicative, it is not desirable to chat to your neighbouring guns on reaching your stand or while waiting for the start. Game has acute hearing. Instead:

i. Make a point of going to your stand quietly. It will probably be marked by a numbered ticket in a cleft stick.

ii. Once there examine the ground a few paces behind it. If it is not already flat make sure that there is nothing likely to trip you up:

a. If the stand is in a ploughed field stamp an even platform for yourself.

b. If it is very muddy and slippery there it is not likely there will be much objection to you moving a short way, but on no account move far.

c. Check that you can see your neighbouring guns on either side and beyond them and know exactly where they are if stationed at an angle to you.

d. If you are stationed at an angle to them, make sure that they see where you are if necessary by waving, but do NOT shout.

e. Make sure also that you know where the birds are likely to be coming from, even if this means that you have to slip quickly across to the next gun and might feel a fool about doing so. You should have been told the plan of campaign, but sometimes it is taken for granted that you will know by divine inspiration.

f. Also make sure that you know where the beaters stops and pickers-up if any, are and are likely to appear from, so that you know exactly where it is safe to shoot.

iii. Work out your safety arcs of fire, i.e. imagine where your pyramids would be and where you could fire safely. Imprint these on your memory.

iv. It is always worth trying a few practice gun mountings and swings before settling down to wait. This will help to relax your muscles and settle you in.

a. You will also be able to check your ranges mentally at the same time.

b. You will be sure your shooting coat is comfortably settled and that you are quite ready.

c. Don't be afraid this will be taken as showing off. It is recognised as sound practice by experienced shots.

v. Give your cartridge bag a good shake and lay it open at your feet. This will bring most of the brass heads to the top and make for easier loading when required.

vi. If you have a dog:

a. If he is reliably steady, as he should be, make him sit at heel, preferably with his back to you so that he can mark the birds that fall behind.

b. If he is not reliably steady, tether him to one of the portable stakes purchasable for the purpose. Do NOT try to shoot with an unsteady dog attached to you on a lead. He is sure to jerk you off aim at a critical moment.

vii. Load your gun, and if you have a shooting stick with you sit yourself down on it quietly with your gaze frontwards above the trees or hedge where you expect the birds to appear.

a. Your gun should either be comfortably held under one arm, the barrels pointing to the ground in front of your feet, or

b. Your barrels should be upright, pointing forwards, the butt resting comfortably against your lower ribs or on your hip.

c. Your gun should NOT be across your knees pointing down the line or parasol fashion over your arm pointing down the line.

d. Do NOT indulge in conversation with your neighbour, even if he comes across to talk to you to continue a conversation you were having beforehand. Make it plain that you feel time for 'coffee-housing' is after the shooting. In no circumstances carry on a shouted conversation. Game is easily alarmed.

viii. When you hear the starting whistle, or the first shot announcing the beginning of the drive:

a. Do NOT leap up from your seat and tense every muscle, even if you do feel an inward sense of anticipation.

b. Stay as completely relaxed as you can and simply keep your gaze in the direction you think the birds are most likely to come.

ix. When you do see the birds coming over you will have plenty of time to stand up, select your bird, mount your gun, swing through and shoot.

a. As far as possible mark where your birds fall.

b. Make particular note of any birds which might be runners, or merely wounded.

    c. Keep a count of the number you have down.

    d. As the beaters approach make a point of taking your shots behind.

x. After the drive is over attend to your own pick-up.

    a. If you have a dog put him on to the runners first, but make sure there is no danger of him disturbing the ground for the next drive. Pick up the birds nearest first and don't let the dog pick them up in the open. It is bad for him and can muddle the count also.

    b. If you do not have a dog, ask someone to put theirs on to the runners for you. Thank him for trying even if his dog fails to find them.

    c. Make sure that you only claim your own birds and not your neighbour's. If there is any doubt allow him the benefit of it. You should not have fired at it together in any case. One of you has failed to observe the rules of shooting, that only birds within your own arc should be shot.

    d. Do NOT waste the keeper's or picker-up's time by asking them to look for birds which you are secretly almost certain are all right but merely feel may have been hit.

    e. Do NOT comment in loud tones on the size of the bag you have shot or the scarcity of birds that came over you.

    f. If possible compliment your neighbours on their shooting and your host on the show of birds. Leave your own performance, good or bad, out of the conversation.

xi. Do NOT forget to unload and to carry your gun broken under your arm between stands so that it can be seen to be unloaded.

Section 4. *At the Butt*

Almost all the points made in Section 3 above are applicable to behaviour in a butt; however there are certain other points to note:

i. If the butt is a round one and safety markers are not provided you would be well advised to put in a couple of twigs to mark the limits of safe arc of fire. In the heat of the moment it is easy to lose a sense of direction and accidentally fire down the line.

ii. Study the moor and try to estimate ranges in advance as well as possible. Keep an eye open for grouse from the moment of arrival and stay alert scanning the ground.

iii. Sometimes a butt will have a patch of heather in front in which birds tend to settle. Even if possibly a little out of range, such birds should be shot at in order to stop them doing so.

iv. Mark any flankers near you with great care as they will be lying concealed in the heather.

v. Remember that it is almost impossible to fire too soon at driven grouse, but:

  a. This only applies to grouse approaching the butt.

  b. Once past the butt long shots should be avoided.

vi. If you see grouse approaching a neighbouring butt which may be out of their view, as quite often happens, give a low warning whistle.

vii. The dog, if you have one, should be outside the butt, but if a prominent colour should be concealed behind the butt.

Section 5. Walking-up

When walking-up game there should again be no question of conversation with the gun on either side. Your whole attention should be on the job in hand.

i. When you approach the starting-point you will line up and take your place in the line according to the number you have picked or have been given:

  a. Spacing between guns and beaters may vary considerably according to the nature of the ground being covered.

  b. Usually there will be at least one beater between each gun and the guns may be as much as 30–40 yards apart in bare grass fields or stubble, though possibly only a matter of 20 yards apart in roots.

ii. Do NOT load your gun before you have taken up your position in the line.

  a. Make sure that it is carried till then under your arm, broken to show that it is unloaded.

  b. When loaded it should be carried under your arm, barrels pointing at the ground, or else over the shoulder, trigger upwards and finger outside the trigger guard, or with butt comfortably on the hip, barrels pointing forwards.

   c. On no account must the gun be carried in line across the body pointing down the line.

iii. Wait for the signal to start walking.

   a. Do NOT just start off when you feel like it.

   b. You must make a point of keeping in line with the gun or beaters on your right and left.

   c. Pay attention to the commands of your host, or organiser, and obey them promptly.

   d. Do NOT consistently forge ahead of the rest of the line. This is an excessively tiresome habit attributed to over-keenness, but generally due to a natural competitive instinct or a desire to hog the shooting. Neither has any place in the shooting field.

   e. Do NOT, on the other hand, consistently lag behind. The pace of the line should be the comfortable pace of the slowest man. Don't hold matters up unnecessarily.

iv. If you have a dog keep him in to heel, unless you have been asked specifically to work him in front.

   a. Do NOT work him in front unless you are sure he is steady to fur.

   b. There is nothing more annoying than seeing a so-called steady dog coursing a hare and raising all the birds for some distance ahead.

v. Try to keep as quiet as possible if you are working your dog in front.

   a. Avoid whistling or shouting unnecessarily.

   b. Game is easily alerted and this will be enough to flush game already running ahead, possibly out of range.

vi. When birds rise in front of or behind the line the entire line should halt automatically.

   a. Only those guns in front of or behind whom the birds rose should fire.

   b. Each gun should take only those birds nearest to him.

   c. In the event of a bird swinging down the line it may be fired at by the gun in front of whom it swings, but no gun should fire down the line after it.

d. When turning to take a bird behind, the gun must of course observe the usual safety precautions, dropping the butt from his shoulder and raising the barrels as he turns, so that they are NOT pointed down the line.

e. If he has not already taken a shot in front, it may just be a question of turning with the barrels pointing down or vertically and taking up his stance facing behind.

vii. Each bird shot should be marked if possible not only by the gun who shot it but by other guns in the line who are not shooting.

a. A mark should be taken, such as a tall tree or pylon, beyond the point where the bird fell. Looking behind, the shot should then mark another point exactly in the opposite direction. He will thus have the line clearly fixed in his mind.

b. Where two people in different parts of the line have thus fixed marks for direction the bird will be found where their lines intersect.

c. In the first instance the line should remain standing while steady dogs are sent forward to pick the birds.

d. A good dog marking the fall should have the ordinary dead bird retrieved promptly, but it is important not to walk forward, as already noted, and so foil the scent. Keep the line at all times.

e. Only if the dog or dogs have failed and there seems a danger of more birds being disturbed by undue whistling or shouting is the line likely to be ordered forward.

f. Then the lines of mark may be tried by those who marked them and the bird looked for by eye. If it is still not found it may well have been a runner.

g. If it is considered certain that it was a dead bird a mark such as a white flag may be left on the spot and the bird searched for later.

h. Sometimes a keeper, or dog handler, is left behind and in such a case great care must be exercised when taking a shot behind subsequently. It is NOT a good plan in general to break the line in this way.

viii. Apart from those birds which have been shot and marked it is advisable to keep an eye on any birds which fly ahead:

 a. To note where they pitch.

 b. In case any were wounded by stray pellets and are seen to fall.

ix. When a shooting party is large enough to cover all the fields entered walking-up is largely a matter of trying to walk into the wind as far as possible and:

 a. Walking to a definite plan: i.e. to drive the birds into roots, where they will hold, or to keep them within the shoot boundaries.

 b. All fields of roots will be walked across the drills, not down them, or the birds will merely run out at the far ends.

 c. When walking through any roots or thick cover it is important that each person should zig-zag, thus covering as much ground as possible and moving the game ahead, *but* the line must keep straight.

x. When the shooting party, as is more often the case, is not large enough to cover a field of roots in one sweep the usual method adopted is:

 a. The line makes a number of sweeps backwards and forwards across the field across the drills.

 b. In such a case it is important not to cut any corners at the end, or leave out the corners of the fields. It is here and at the very edge of the field that the birds are most likely to be found.

 c. If these corners or edges are not fully walked out the birds will remain clapped down and hidden.

xi. Another and often very successful way of dealing with a large field with only a few guns is:

 a. The line sweeps round the field clockwise in a circle.

 b. The centre of the field is then taken in one sweep across, or variations may be made on this, i.e. two circles made or a figure-of-eight.

 c. By this method the coveys can be successfully broken up, making for interesting shooting.

Section 6. Dogging

It should be appreciated that dogging is almost a separate sport compared with walking-up or shooting driven birds.

i. The important factor here, fully equal to the shooting, is the pleasure afforded by watching the dog work.

    a. The rhythmic quartering action of the good working dog and the eagerness of his questing are in themselves a pleasure to watch.

    b. Each movement of the dog's head, each wave of the stern (i.e. wag of the tail), should have its separate meaning to those who understand.

    c. A half check may be cold scent of birds, an indulgent wave of the stern a note that a rabbit or hare has been there. A slow approach and stiffening, or full point and rigid stance, means business.

ii. The number of guns shooting over dogs is probably not more than five and more customarily limited to two.

iii. Conversation, as in any form of shooting, is to be kept to a minimum.

iv. The guns line up behind the dogs with the dog handlers in the line, if they are not themselves shooting.

v. Ground game, or low shots at birds, must be taken with the greatest care for the dogs' safety.

vi. On a dog coming on point the guns nearest on either side should move towards the point.

    a. If necessary the handler should break line and get up with his dog, but not passing in front of either gun.

    b. As the dog draws-on, i.e. moves forward on point, the guns on either side should advance level with the dog and the handler.

    c. This advance may go on for as much as a hundred yards on a moor, or farther, but with partridges or pheasants in stubble or roots should not last long.

vii. The shot at dogging early in the season is almost invariably what the shooting man cares to make it.

    a. It may be taken at close range, or:

    b. It may be allowed reasonable range and turned into a sporting shot.

viii. Later in the season the gun shooting over dogs must be ready to take his shots the instant he notes the dog give him warning of the presence of game.

ix. The gun out dogging is likely to walk a much greater mileage than either the gun walking-up or the gun at driven game, but he is not likely to notice it unduly at the time.

x. Although the bag is not likely to be as large as that in either of the other forms of shooting, it is particularly true to say that this is no measure of the sport or the enjoyment, but:

    a. It must be reiterated that the shooting is the lesser part of the sport.

    b. The newcomer to this form of shooting, however good a shot, must not expect to understand it, or necessarily enjoy it, unless he also understands the behaviour of birds and dogs.

Section 7. After Shooting

At the end of the day's sport, regardless of what kind of shooting it has been, there are certain points which should not be forgotten or overlooked:

i. If you have a dog with you he should be your first care:

    a. If he is wet see that he has a good rub down with a towel or sacking you have brought for the purpose.

    b. Bed him down comfortably, either in straw if you have a kennel compartment in your car, or on a blanket to save your seats and to give him a bit of comfort.

    c. If you are going to be any length of time it may be as well to give him a light meal and a drink if he wants one.

    d. Do NOT just let him roam around until you are ready.

    e. Do NOT just shove him in the boot, or back of the car, and forget about him, wet and cold.

    f. Do NOT leave him, especially wet and cold, with any game. However good a gun dog this is not a wise combination and you may find him busy eating them on your return.

    g. Even if he has been thoroughly disobedient this was probably your fault for not training him properly in the first case. Look after him now and make sure he is given plenty of training before taking him out again.

ii. The gun should be put away, having first made certain that it was unloaded and preferably:

   a. Having quickly pulled it through and removed the worst of the day's dirt from the barrels.

   b. Taken to pieces and packed away in its travelling case.

   This way there cannot be one of those ghastly accidents with a loaded gun in the back of a car.

iii. The bag should be inspected and if there has been a sweep-stake on it, or on the head of vermin shot, you may as well check on how far you were out, also:

   a. Take the opportunity of complimenting your host and of thanking the head keeper for the day.

   b. If you do not know what the local form is as regards tipping him, check with your host or one of the other guns who has shot there before.

   c. Tips will always vary according to the day and bag. They should in any event represent in some degree your personal satisfaction and thanks for the organisation and work which has gone to make up the day.

   d. What you give over a minimum is largely your own affair.

   e. Failure to tip is another of those reasons for not receiving a second invitation to shoot.

iv. After all this has been attended to the day may be discussed round the fire and over a drink, but:

   a. Remember to comment favourably, if you can, on your neighbour's shooting, not your own.

   b. Do not complain and do not crab, whatever your grounds may be for doing so.

   c. However well you shoot, if you disregard these points you will never be a sportsman.

v. On your return home a letter of thanks to your host is a courtesy which will be appreciated.

BOOK 3

The Background of Shooting

PART I

WEATHER, SCENT, GAME BEHAVIOUR AND MARKING, ETC.

Section 1. Clouds and the Weather

It is important to know the various clouds and their likely effects on the weather:

i. Cirrus: Usually found from 27,000 feet to 50,000 feet. Known more generally as Mare's Tails.

    a. Delicate, feathery clouds, like locks of hair, sometimes in fan shapes.

    b. The wind on the earth's surface will eventually follow the direction in which they are moving.

    c. If streaks of cirrus form a V shape pointing north or west, wind and possibly rain can be expected from that direction.

    d. If the streaks of cirrus become greyer and darker, rain can be expected.

    e. If they fade into a dark blue sky, good weather can be expected.

ii. Cirro-Stratus: Usually about 29,000 feet.

    a. Generally appear as groups of small clouds like shoals of fish.

    b. May appear as a thin white sheet of cloud thicker in the middle than the edges.

iii. Cirro-Cumulus: Usually found from 10,000 feet to 23,000 feet.

    a. Consist of small round bundles of clouds, like wool.

    b. When dotted around the sky at intervals mean fine weather.

    c. When close together mean rain and storm.

iv. Cumulus: Usually found from 4,500 feet to 6,000 feet.

    a. Look like large wool packs.

    b. Very typical dry weather clouds: BUT

c. If they persist towards evening they are usually a sign of rain.

v. Cumulo-Nimbus: Vary in height from 4,500 feet to 24,000 feet.

    a. Are vast cloud formations, usually white on top, copper coloured lower down, and dark black and threatening below.

    b. The typical and well-known storm cloud.

vi. Nimbus: Usually from 3,000 feet to 6,500 feet.

    a. Is a continuous layer of dark grey cloud.

    b. Familiarly known as the rain cloud and needing little introduction or description in this country.

vii. Stratus: May be from ground level to 3,500 feet.

    a. Horizontal layers of clouds. Sometimes fog or mist.

    b. When the sun rises through steadily disappearing layers of Stratus mist it means a fine day to come.

viii. The following points may be noted:

    a. Clouds banked together in the west usually mean rain to come.

    b. Clouds with ragged broken edges usually mean rain and wind.

    c. When the clouds have clear-cut edges the likelihood is that they will pass without rain.

    d. Soft delicate clouds in the sky usually indicate fine weather and moderate breezes.

Section 2. The Wind and the Weather

Certain points about wind and weather are worth noting.

i. A strong veering wind:

    a. The wind veers when moving with the sun from east to south and west, or clockwise.

    b. Will usually die away and means settled weather.

ii. A backing wind:

    a. The wind backs when moving against the sun from west to south and east, or anti-clockwise.

    b. Will usually increase and means unsettled weather.

iii. When the wind is blowing in the opposite direction to the movement of the clouds:

   a. Usually indicates a change in the weather.

   b. If it has been wet and windy, will improve.

   c. If it has been fine, will probably change to wet and windy.

iv. Wind is measured by the Beaufort Scale as follows:

Beaufort Scale	Description of wind and effects	Approximate speed, m.p.h.
0	Calm: When smoke rises vertically and light twigs on trees unmoving	0
1	Light airs: When smoke drifts from chimney and topmost twigs of tree just move	2
2	Light breeze: Wind felt on face and topmost twigs of tree seen to be moving	5
3	Gentle breeze: When leaves and small twigs are moved constantly	10
4	Moderate breeze: When bushes sway and small branches of trees move	15
5	Fresh breeze: Small trees begin to sway and their tops seen in motion	20
6	Strong breeze: Large branches seen moving and wind whistles through trees	30
7	Moderate Gale: Whole trees seen swaying. Distinct effect on person when walking. Shooting birds on wing impractical if wind behind them. May be suitable for wildfowling	35
8	Fresh Gale: Breaks twigs off trees. Unsuitable for any shooting other than wildfowling.	40

Section 3. Sunrise, Sunset, Rainbows and the Weather

A reasonably accurate weather forecast can usually be made from the following points:

i. Sunrise:

   a. If there is a clear unclouded horizon when the sun rises settled weather can be expected for twenty-four hours.

   b. A red sky in the morning implies unsettled weather for twenty-four hours.

   c. When the sun rises above a bank of clouds it usually means unsettled weather.

     d. A grey sky in the morning may mean fine weather. N.B.: But note the type of clouds. If Nimbus, expect rain.

ii. Sunset:

     a. A red sky at sunset, whether cloudy or clear, implies settled weather for twenty-four hours.

     b. A grey overcast sky in the evening implies unsettled weather to come.

     c. A watery yellow sunset means rain.

     d. A bright but yellowy sunset usually means wind.

iii. Rainbows:

     a. A rainbow in the morning usually means wet weather to come during the day.

     b. A rainbow in the evening generally means fine weather to follow.

Section 4. Weather Notes

The following points regarding the weather are worth noting:

i. The prevailing wind in the British Isles is south-west.

     a. This strikes the mountain districts of Ireland, Cornwall, Wales and Scotland first.

     b. It is warm air heavy with moisture from the Atlantic.

     c. On hitting the high ground it parts with the moisture in the form of rain.

     d. It then descends to the lower warmer air on the east coast and takes up moisture.

     e. It is for this reason the east coast is drier than the west.

ii. Rain before seven, fine before eleven.

     a. The explanation for the general truth of this saying is that the belts of bad weather crossing the country are usually about four or five hours in width.

     b. It therefore takes just about this period to pass over any particular place.

iii. A patch of blue sky 'large enough to make a pair of pants' in a grey sky usually means the weather will improve.

iv. Pronouncedly clear visibility at a distance—

     a. When distant hills are unusually clearly seen in daytime;

b. When stars at night are noticeably twinkling and visible; usually indicates unsettled weather.

v. Reactions of various animals should be noted:

   a. Gulls in unusual quantities inland mean the approach of a storm.

   b. Cattle huddle together on the approach of a storm, but lie down in preference to moving about before rain.

   c. Swallows fly low when rain is coming.

   d. Game will be hard to find and move when a storm is approaching.

vi. The following definitions should be understood:

   a. An open winter: i.e. mild weather with rain rather than snow.

   b. A hard winter: i.e. hard, prolonged cold weather with heavy frost and snow.

   c. A black frost: i.e. an intense and deep frost by which vegetation is blackened.

   d. A white frost: i.e. a hoar frost composed mostly of surface frost of frozen dew. N.B.: After several days' hoar frost it usually rains.

Section 5. Scent

Every animal, including man, has its own particular and highly individual smell:

i. This smell may vary:

   a. With the type of animal, as above.

   b. With the sex, or age, of the animal.

   c. With the state of mind of the animal, i.e. at rest and at ease, or alarmed and alert, or afraid.

   d. With the activities of the animal, i.e. sleeping, feeding, moving fast or slow.

   e. With the condition of the animal, i.e. fit or sickly.

ii. This smell, or scent, is the result of excretions from the glands of the animals.

   a. The extent of these excretions varies, as above.

   b. Microscopic particles of these excretions form the scent.

iii. These microscopic particles of scent are conveyed in two ways:

    a. By contact with the ground, or any object, whereby these particles may cling to the ground, or the object, i.e. brushing against grass.

    b. By the passage of air over the animal wafting these particles with the wind.

iv. Specifically therefore scent may be referred to as:

    a. Ground scent.

    b. Air scent.

v. Gun dogs are sometimes misleadingly classified therefore as:

    a. Ground scenters or foot scenters, i.e. retrievers and spaniels.

    b. Air scenters, i.e. pointers and setters.

BUT:

    c. This takes no account of pointer-retrievers, or of spaniels or retrievers which point, i.e. dogs which clearly are both ground and air scenters at different times.

vi. The well-trained and experienced dog should be able:

    a. To find and follow either ground or air scent as is necessary.

    b. To differentiate at the same time between the various types of game, i.e. fur or feather and the variety of each.

    c. To distinguish at the same time between the various conditions of game, i.e. whether wounded, or dead, or untouched.

vii. There is nothing unusual about a dog trained in this way:

    a. It is the basis of dogging and all hunting.

    b. In the wild state the fox and the wolf must learn the same lessons if they wish to eat.

viii. Remember that game can also smell man.

Section 6. *The Effect of Wind, Weather and Soil on Scent*

Clearly the microscopic particles which compose scent must be affected in different ways by different weather conditions and different soil conditions.

i. Both air and soil should contain a certain degree of moisture to provide good conditions for the scent particles to remain easily identifiable.

    a. Soil and air should also be about the same temperature to keep the particles of scent more or less static.

    b. If the temperature of the air is higher than the soil the scent tends to rise.

    c. If the temperature of the soil is lower than that of the air the scent tends to remain at ground level.

ii. Extremes of weather conditions tend to be bad for scent:

    a. Too wet and the scent may be washed away.

    b. Too dry and the scent may disappear too quickly, or fail to lie.

    c. Too windy as above.

iii. Bad scenting conditions are:

    a. When the ground is hard and the air dry, scent usually does not lie.

    b. Ploughland with a drying wind is poor for scent.

    c. Frost or decaying leaves are bad for scenting.

    d. Warm sunshine and thaw conditions are usually poor.

    e. Certain road surfaces are very bad.

    f. Where roots have been frosted and smell strongly, or are very dry and dusty.

iv. Reasonable scenting conditions may be had:

    a. With a southerly or light west wind, conditions are likely to be quite good.

    b. Dew if not too heavy, mist and fog, appear to make little difference to scent.

    c. Scent usually lies high in frosty conditions, i.e. the scent particles rise slightly. N.B.: Hence the term 'breast high scent'. It is breast high to the hound.

    d. On grass land, or heathy land scent is usually quite good depending on weather conditions.

v. Dogs may be at fault on a scent even in apparently good scenting conditions for a number of reasons:

    a. Lack of 'nose', or ability to scent.

    b. This may be permanent, in which case the dog should not be kept, except as a pet. It is useless as a gun dog.

    c. This may be temporary, due to the dog being off-colour, or to dusty conditions, e.g. in roots as above, or to unsuitable feeding, e.g. cheese sandwiches at lunch.

d. This may be due to too much game, i.e. conflicting scents and lack of experience or ability to follow them.

e. A change of soil conditions, as above, may lead to loss of scent.

f. Backtracking, or doubling back by the animal, or the trail being broken.

g. Following the heel scent, or wrong direction, back to starting-point. A fault of inexperience.

Section 7. *The Effects of the Weather on Game*

In normal weather conditions most game has its particular range of territory from which it is unlikely to stray without due reason; i.e. in search of mate, food, or shelter from weather or persecution by man or other predators.

i. The effect of exceptional weather conditions.

a. In exceptionally hot and dry conditions game birds may be expected to remain near water and shade.

b. In exceptionally wet conditions they may usually be found in the lee of some shelter in the open. No game likes the dripping conditions of wet trees or roots.

c. In exceptionally windy or snowy conditions they may be expected in shelter belts of trees, or hedges, or in hollows out of the direct blast.

ii. The very worst conditions of wind, rain or snow are seldom enough to drive a game bird off a nest once sitting on eggs.

iii. The worst possible time for game bird mortality due to weather is:

a. When the youngsters are still unable to fly, very wet weather for any length of time is extremely bad.

b. Exceptionally dry weather, i.e. a drought, during the same period can also be very bad.

iv. An extremely hard winter when the birds have not had any feeding will result in a lot of deaths then or in the following spring, also in failure to breed.

v. When partridges or grouse have paired the effect of a sudden cold spell may be to make them form coveys or packs again.

vi. Prolonged periods of driving rain, combined with windy conditions early in the season, will result in:

    a. Late broods will be decimated.

    b. The birds will become wild and difficult to drive or shoot very early on in the season.

vii. Driving rain, or high winds overnight the day before shooting, mean:

    a. The birds will have had a disturbed night and they will be sitting out in the open to get dry.

    b. They will be alert and suspicious, ready to fly at the first sign of danger.

    c. They will rise wild and far out and will prove difficult to drive in the right direction.

viii. A sudden cold snap and frost overnight the night before shooting will result in:

    a. The birds tending to sit tight.

    b. They will be easier to drive.

    c. The bag should be correspondingly larger.

ix. Any wind over Force 5 makes shooting very much more difficult:

    a. The birds will be moving proportionately faster.

    b. They will tend to have an awkward curl on them, making every shot a great deal harder.

x. Apart from the obvious disadvantages to man and gun, game shooting in prolonged heavy rain is not recommended:

    a. Because birds are unlikely to fly well even if they can be found.

    b. Scent will be non-existent.

xi. Exceptional heat is also unsuitable for shooting:

    a. Because birds are often reluctant to fly, sitting tight until forced up:

    b. Scent is non-existent.

xii. Due regard must be had to the likes and dislikes of the various game birds, their breeding and feeding habits:

    a. After a prolonged wet spell when water meadows have been flooded, snipe and duck may be expected.

   b. A period of prolonged freezing is likely to close up all the
   ponds and flashes for duck and snipe formed by the flood-
   ing. They will then move to river and open water, i.e.
   flowing water.
   c. Woodcock and snipe will usually be found near soft or
   splashy ground suitable for their bills. This may vary as
   above.

Section 8. The Effects of Shot on Game

The game shot's object will always be to take each shot with
sufficient skill to kill the bird cleanly at once. Inevitably this may
not always be achieved and he should learn to distinguish a dead
bird from one that is winged, or otherwise affected by the shot,
as follows:

i. A bird shot stone dead—
   a. From behind: may be seen to fold its wings, possibly to
   drop both legs as well, and fall instantaneously.
   b. From the side or front: may be seen to fold its wings and
   turn into a ball of feathers in mid-air. Or if hit entirely in
   the head or beak it may cartwheel in mid-air. Again will be
   seen to fall instantaneously.

ii. A 'Towered' bird:
   a. Is one which has supposedly a pellet in the lung or spine.
   b. This happens occasionally and has the effect of causing it
   to beat the air with its wings, flying higher and higher as
   either its lungs fill with blood or the nerves react.
   c. It sometimes reaches a considerable height and distance
   before dropping vertically stone dead.
   d. Frequently found on its back and often has little scent.

iii. A winged bird:
   a. A bird which has had one wing broken is likely to fall with
   the head still up.
   b. May otherwise be mistaken for a dead bird due to the
   abruptness of its fall.
   c. May be seen to get up on landing and start running towards the nearest cover.
   d. When only a wing-tip has been affected the bird may be
   seen to glide to the ground, sometimes at quite a distance.

    e. Wing-tipped birds may often be seen to start running before actually landing.

    f. When badly winged, unlikely to recover; and a dog should be set on the spot where seen to land as soon as possible.

iv. A winged bird also hit in the body:

    a. If a bird is seen to drop winged and feathers are seen to fall from the body; or:

    b. If a bird is seen to plane down after feathers have been knocked out of it by the shot, it has been hit in the body as well as the wing.

    c. The spot where it landed should be marked. It is not likely to run far.

    d. It will probably be found lying up in the nearest hedge or cover.

v. When a fallen bird is seen to bounce up and flutter its wings:

    a. This is NOT a runner.

    b. It is stone dead, but has probably been hit in the head, or:

    c. Is a 'towered' bird with one or both wings broken. In either case will be picked up where last seen: dead.

vi. The bird which is seen to wince, or flutter its wings rapidly as the shot is fired:

    a. This is sometimes particularly noticeable in the case of overhead shots, where the body is exposed, but:

    b. May also be seen in crossing shots and less often in going away shots at an angle.

    c. This is a bird to watch carefully especially if feathers are seen to fly, as the chances are that after flying apparently normally for 200–300 yards or more it will suddenly fall dead.

    d. It may be seen to flutter up to a perch, or apparently land with a slightly more laboured beat than normal, or it may simply fall dead.

    e. If in any doubt about such a bird it is advisable to go to where it was last seen. It is often to be found stone dead.

vii. The bird which puts a leg down:

    a. If feathers are seen to fly this probably means it has been hit in the body as well and it should be watched as above.

>   *b.* If the bird puts both legs down but flies on it is not likely to
>   rise again and should be marked to the point of landing.
>   *c.* No effort should be spared to find a bird with both legs
>   down as it cannot possibly live.

viii. The stunned bird:

>   *a.* A bird which is merely stunned by a pellet glancing from
>   the beak or skull and not otherwise damaged may show
>   remarkable powers of recovery.
>   *b.* It may crash to the ground from a considerable height and
>   recover on the ground to fly away before being picked up.
>   *c.* Birds so affected have been known to fly out of a game bag
>   at the end of a day.
>   *d.* It is even possible for such a bird to cartwheel down,
>   breaking small branches, and to recover again 6 feet from
>   ground and fly on.

ix. Ground game:

>   *a.* The hare which is seen to leap as the shot is fired is almost
>   certainly hit in the lungs.
>   *b.* It will be found stone dead within a quarter of a mile if a
>   dog is set on the trail after a lapse of ten minutes or so.
>   *c.* It is not advisable to set the dog on the line too soon as
>   this merely encourages the hare to run with a last spurt of
>   energy and it will then fall dead, but will possibly be lost
>   to the bag.
>   *d.* The hare or rabbit moving at speed when properly shot in
>   the head will generally cartwheel over stone dead.
>   *e.* If seen to be hit behind, the second barrel should be used at
>   once.

Section 9. *Marking the Fall*

Whenever possible the fall of game should be marked, especially
if there is any doubt about it being cleanly killed, i.e. if there is
any possibility of it being a runner.

i. The actual method of marking may have to be varied to suit
the circumstances and conditions and must vary with the
nature of the ground.

ii. One of the simplest methods is by use of a prominent object close to the point where the bird fell, i.e. a bird falling in a root field might be marked as close to a large thistle, or similar marker.

iii. Alternatively a bird may be estimated as having fallen at about 40 yards range and a marker taken as to line, i.e. in line with a telegraph pole in the hedge, or a similar prominent marker for line.

iv. A combination of marking for fall and for direction is sometimes both possible and desirable, i.e. the fall is marked as near the thistle in line with the telegraph pole.

    a. By this method there is less danger of losing the marker for fall, i.e. changing thistles.

    b. It is worth turning round to take a second marker for direction in the opposite direction. Then the line of fall is fixed between the two markers.

v. A runner should be marked from the point of fall and if possible the direction in which it started running should be noted, so that a dog may be set on the right line as soon as possible.

    a. It is important that the scent should not be foiled by anyone walking over the ground prior to the dog being set on it.

    b. The position of any other birds down nearby should be noted so that should the dog pick them it can still be sent on after the runner.

vi. The 'towered' bird is often extremely difficult and most deceptive to mark.

    a. To mark a towering bird effectively it is a good plan to go down on one knee, or bend down to about waist level, to watch its fall.

    b. This will give you a false horizon and a second angle of view, helping you to fix both direction and distance more easily and accurately.

    c. It is worth remembering that it will almost always appear to be a great deal farther away than it really is. If you estimate it as having fallen about a 100 yards out, the chances are that it is really much nearer to 60. Such birds can sometimes be a long way out, however.

vii. When driven birds are really coming over fast it may only be possible to memorise the number down and the general position. Here a dog which can mark really well (and it is astonishing how good they can become with practice) is a tremendous asset.

Section 10. *Dealing with Wounded Game*

When the game has been marked and retrieved successfully the shot should know how to deal with it humanely and cleanly if it is not dead:

i. Game birds may be humanely despatched with special pliers, which are very effective, or by using a fisherman's priest.

    a. If your fingers are strong enough the skull may be crushed by pressing the crossed thumbs down on the back of the skull. With young game it is simple, with older and larger game not so easy.

    b. As quick, though scarcely as clean, is the old fowler's method of biting the skull between the teeth.

ii. If the bird is held by the body a sharp rap of the back of the skull and neck over the toe of the boot will usually be quite sufficient.

    a. Do NOT rap the bird on the gun, or alternatively:

    b. Try to beat it to death with the butt.

iii. Swinging the bird round in circles while holding on to the head will usually result in the body flying off at a tangent and the bloody head being left in your hand. It is NOT recommended.

iv. Breaking the neck by holding the body in one hand and applying a pressure to the neck may well have the same effect. The head is liable to come away in the hand resulting in a gory mess.

v. Hares should be held by the hind legs with a foot across their necks. Steady pressure may then be applied until the neck is broken.

Section 11. *Sexing and Ageing*

When examining the bag it is worth while being able to sex and age the game reasonably accurately and quickly. As a rough guide:

i. Sex can usually be readily decided by the descriptions given in the ensuing sections on game (Part 2).

ii. Young game birds of almost all species can be gauged by the softness of their skulls or breastbones when squeezed. When held up by the lower mandible their weight will bend it.

iii. Young birds can generally be noted by the pointed tips of their primaries. In older birds these are invariably rounded.

iv. Length of spurs in cocks, general hoariness in hens and heavier weight in both sexes are signs of age.

v. A match probed into the bursa, a small blind passage on the upper side of the vent, is a more scientific determiner of age. If it goes in more than a quarter of an inch it is a young bird. Effective on partridges, grouse and pheasants.

vi. In ground game the lower jaw will readily squeeze together in the young. The ears of young ground game will tear very readily.

PART 2

THE GAME

Section 1. The Red Grouse

Lagopus scoticus once thought unique to Great Britain but now widely accepted as the British variant of Willow Grouse.

i. Habitat and Distribution: The habitat, as noted earlier, is on moors chiefly from Yorkshire northwards throughout the greater part of Scotland.

ii. Seasons:

 a. Shooting, or Open, Season from 12th August to 10th December inclusive.

 b. Breeding, or Close, Season from 11th December to 11th August inclusive.

iii. Average Appearance, Markings and Size (Male and Female):

 a. A reddish-brown, or buff, barred or spotted bird, which moults twice a year and has considerable local variation of plumage and colouring. Feathered legs are noticeable.

 b. Chestnut red feathers are usually more distinct on the chin, throat and breast of the cock. Hens are more liable to be barred, or of lighter colouring. Can be hard to sex except during the breeding season.

 c. Average size about fifteen inches from tip of beak to tail and weight about $1\frac{1}{2}$ lb., but Yorkshire birds weigh up to 2 lb. Hens are slightly smaller.

iv. Call: A throaty gurgle, resembling 'Go-back, Go-back', but often notable for silent flight.

v. Breeding Habits:

 a. Will pair and choose territory as early as November/December and are amongst the earliest game birds to nest.

 b. The number of eggs laid may vary from 6–12, but up to 15–17 known.

 c. Incubation usually starts in early May and lasts from 24–27 days.

146

vi. Principal Foods:

   a. Young ling heather shoots are the foremost food.

   b. Blaeberry, crowberry, cranberry (and most other berries), insects and oats, etc., also are included in the diet at times.

   c. They require considerable quantities of grit, which is taken into the gizzard and remains there for some time, a few being ejected each day.

vii. Diseases to which they are notably susceptible are:

   a. *Trichostrongylus pergracilis:* a tiny parasitic worm indigenous to grouse, which multiplies rapidly and proves fatal when the grouse is in poor condition due to lack of feeding, i.e. after a severe winter, or when the heather has been frosted, or attacked by heather beetle. N.B.: Its life cycle is formed by passing through the grouse droppings into the heather, then re-ingested.

   b. Coccidiosis. A parasitic infection causing acute diarrhoea and death of chicks. Common also in other game birds.

viii. Flight:

   a. Liable to be deceptive, because:

   b. Periods of intense activity of the wings are punctuated with gliding on set pinions.

   c. This may impart an up-and-down, or bobbing, effect in flight; also seldom entirely straight. There is usually a slight tendency to curl accentuated by any wind.

ix. Packing:

   a. Grouse will start to form packs early in the season, varying with the locality and circumstance, usually by October.

   b. They form packs of 100–150, or over double that number.

   c. The sexes are segregated: Cocks and hens.

   d. There are invariably single old birds on every moor which do not pack.

x. Migration:

   a. It is now an accepted fact that grouse do migrate from their home moors on occasions. It may happen at any time.

   b. Reasons may be:
   Exceptional weather conditions, i.e. severe winter, or a bad drought during the summer on the moor.

Disease, or severe frosting or burning of the heather, i.e. a shortage of feeding.

Undue persecution, i.e. harrying by man (hikers during breeding season, etc.) or other predators, i.e. eagles, buzzards, foxes; or by older grouse of young when overstocked on the moor.

In short, any interference with food supplies or way of life may cause a moor to be deserted temporarily.

c. Migration from one moor to another may be purely temporary, due to a desire for a change of feeding, i.e. an attractive patch of blaeberries ripening, or similar reason.

d. Whatever the reason, whether temporary or permanent, migration can suddenly empty one moor and double the population on another.

e. Distances of migrations are uncertain, but may well be considerable. Grouse range normally over a very wide area. Ringed grouse have been recovered at distances of 20 miles and more.

xi. Variety of grouse and moors:

a. It is notable that grouse themselves vary widely in colour, appearance, type and taste, from north to south, or even moor to moor. Much must depend on feeding.

b. Even more than low ground shootings every moor is entirely different from the next and this appears to be reflected in the grouse themselves.

xii. Methods of shooting:

a. Walking-up is usually only practised on very small moors. It is much less common than on low ground shoots.

b. The choice usually lies between shooting driven grouse or dogging.

xiii. Points to note when shooting:

a. Numbers can be very difficult to deal with when first faced with a large pack streaming over the butt.

b. It is very easy for the beginner to lose his nerve and fire 'into the brown', rather than picking each bird carefully. N.B.: Often two or more may fall to one shot, but this is undesirable as it casts doubt on ability to pick a bird correctly.

c. It is the silence of the grouse's sudden appearance which may also unnerve the beginner.

d. The grouse may unexpectedly appear 40 yards away, then be past and gone before he has appreciated the fact.

e. The bobbing flight, sinking into the heather, out of sight at intervals as they approach is also difficult even for the experienced shot.

f. Hesitation at driven grouse is fatal and often dangerous, as it may result in a swing past into the danger zone of next butt. Snap shooting is almost imperative.

g. Shooting up or down hill, or at birds beneath the level of the gun, can add to the difficulties, as well as the fact that many of the birds will be curling.

h. Apart from the fact that there is usually no means of estimating height or range the high grouse is usually an easier shot than most others.

i. The grouse in October is a very different and much more difficult bird to shoot compared with the grouse in August.

Section 2. *The Ptarmigan*

Lagopus mutus is probably one of the least shot game birds in the country.

i. Habitat and Distribution: The habitat is usually above the 2,000 foot mark, above tree level (except in the Hebrides), amongst the rocky stones and boulders of the Scottish Highlands.

ii. Seasons:

    a. Shooting, or Open, Season from 12th August to 10th December inclusive.

    b. Breeding, or Close, Season from 11th December to 11th August inclusive.

iii. Average Appearance, Markings and Size:

    a. Like its cousin the grouse, constantly moulting and liable to considerable local variations. It also has feathered legs.

    b. In summer the male is white chested and white winged, body grey merging with blacks and scarlet eye wattle. The female is grey with buff tones. Both tone to white in the winter.

    c. Average size is about 14 inches from the tip of the beak to tail and weight about 1¼ lb. Slightly smaller than the red grouse.

iv. Call is a croaking sound; but ptarmigan are notable chiefly for their silent flight from amongst the rocks they closely resemble.

v. Breeding Habits:

    a. They will pair as early as red grouse, but nest later.

    b. The nest usually consists of a scrape in the rocks containing 5–9 eggs.

    c. The incubation period is similar to the grouse, 24–27 days, usually in June.

vi. Principal Foods:

    a. Leaves of dwarf sallow and birch. Various mosses, etc.

    b. Blaeberry, cranberry, crowberry, when available.

    c. Also consumes large quantities of grit.

viii. Points to note:

    a. Dogging or walking-up are likely to be the only methods of shooting. It is seldom practicable to drive them.

    b. Where stalking is the principal preoccupation ptarmigan are seldom shot.

    c. Climbing around the high tops is no child's play and with a gun requires considerable care; also local knowledge highly desirable.

    d. Ptarmigan are reputed sometimes to be extremely tame and refuse to fly at all. No sportsman, of course, would shoot them in such circumstances.

    e. It is more probable that after an exhausting climb to ptarmigan ground all that will be seen is several distant rocks suddenly and silently taking wing and vanishing over the crest of a hill out of range.

    f. Ptarmigan are amazingly well camouflaged and appear prepared to fly into outer space, i.e. across to a neighbouring mountain top, though more often simply sticking to the contours of the hill itself.

    g. Shooting is then a matter of snap shooting and the retrieve may be a matter of considerable difficulty. Care must be had for the dog's safety as well as human's.

h. Little appears to be known about ptarmigan's movements. They do come down from the high tops in very severe weather, but seldom seen save by shepherds and ghillies. They probably have as wide, if not wider, range of movement as grouse for similar reasons. Seldom recorded south of Highland Line, a covey was noted in Dumfriesshire in 1784.

i. Their only predator to any extent would appear to be the golden eagle.

Section 3. *The Black Grouse*

Lyrurus tetrix, more generally known as blackgame; divided by sex into blackcock and greyhen.

i. Habitat and Distribution: The habitat is the edges of moors, forests, heaths and marshes; once widely distributed over south, including heaths of Surrey, but habitats as well as numbers sadly diminishing. Now restricted to Devon and Cornwall in the south and from both sides of the Border northwards.

ii. Seasons:

a. Shooting, or Open, Season from 20th August to 10th December inclusive.

b. Breeding, or Close, Season from 11th December to 19th August inclusive.

iii. Average Appearance, Markings and Size (Male and Female):

a. The cock is a large glossy black bird with a lyre-shaped tail, and white underneath. The hen is smaller, light brown, resembling a grouse, except for the white wing bar.

b. Average size of the male is 21 inches from the tip of the beak to the tail. Female, 16 inches. The cocks weight 3½–4 lb.; the hens 2¼–3 lb.

iv. Call: When mating, a remarkable gobbling musical sound. Otherwise notable for silent flight, though gobbling chuckling sound may be made as warning sometimes.

v. Breeding Habits:

a. Polygamous: perform 'lek' or courtship dance in special 'lekking' or breeding grounds in April. Cocks dance in a circle and display lyre tails over their backs to the hens. Cocks fight: hens watch: winner takes all.

b. Nest usually contains from 6–10 eggs. Choice of site often rushy, mere type of ground.

c. Incubation usually starts at the end of April and lasts from 24–27 days.

vi. Principal Foods:

a. Difficult to pin down as practically omnivorous as regards insects and vegetables.

b. Will admittedly sometimes eat the tips of young shoots from trees, hence are disliked by the Forestry Commission, but this is probably very minor damage.

vii. Flight:

a. Has a slower wing beat than grouse, but moves two or three times as fast.

b. Is liable to fly very high and also to turn and circle back over the same ground.

viii. Methods of Shooting:

a. Rarely the principal object of any shooting day, since may live on lower edges of moor, or above on rocky fringes. Very hard to drive.

b. May be shot dogging, but old blackgame a match in cunning for most dogs and liable to run well ahead before taking wing.

c. Generally shot in the course of a drive for grouse or capercaillie.

ix. Points to note when shooting:

a. Early in the grouse season young blackgame are liable to appear and greyhens are easily mistaken for grouse by the beginner, but note the differences in flight above.

b. This is a mistake easily enough made, but may be subject to a local penalty, varying from 50p to a bottle of whisky.

c. Young blackgame may be easy shots until well into September and should be left until later if possible. There is no sport in shooting youngsters however large.

d. The speed of blackgame is most deceptive and can only be fully appreciated when seen against the flight of grouse.

When taking a shot remember this point and swing accordingly faster or the shot will be miles behind.

e. Although they look an easy large mark they are far more difficult to shoot than may be anticipated. Also they are liable to be much higher than is imagined, or farther away.

f. Range can be difficult to estimate because of size.

g. If you have No. 5s or No. 4s use them and don't take long shots.

Section 4. *The Capercaillie, or Capercailzie*

Tetrao urogallus is the largest game bird found in this country. Of the Grouse family.

i. Habitat and Distribution: Strictly a bird of the pine woods, although often found on the edges of forest and moor. Supposedly extinct in the early nineteenth century, it was re-introduced in Perthshire by Lord Breadalbane and Sir Thomas Fowell Buxton in 1837 when a breeding stock from Sweden was imported. Today it has spread far north of Inverness and as far south as Dumfries.

ii. Seasons:

a. Shooting, or Open, Season from 1st October to 31st January inclusive.

b. Breeding, or Close, Season from 1st February to 30th September inclusive.

iii. Average Appearance, Markings and Size (Male and Female):

a. The cock is a very large bird with greeny-black breast and olive-brown back, with prominent patch of white where wing joins body. Scarlet eye wattle, prominent beak. Quite unmistakable when full grown.

b. Hen is similar to red grouse and greyhen, but larger. And has rounded tail and rufous patch on chest.

c. Average size of male is 34 inches from tip of beak to tail. Female 24 inches. Cocks weigh up to 12 lb., hens 7–8 lb.

iv. Call: Notable for silence except during mating when the cock reputedly makes a sound like a cork being pulled.

v. Breeding Habits:

a. Polygamous and the cock will court his following of hens

with a somewhat similar display to the lekking of the blackcock, only a solo performance.

  b. The hen will wander off to nest on her own, sometimes a matter of miles.

  c. This and the polygamous habits of them all can lead to crosses with blackgame and pheasants.

  d. The nest is usually no more than a scrape in the edge of forest in scrub undergrowth.

  e. The number of eggs may vary from 5–10, usually laid in early May. Incubation takes from 26–29 days.

vi. Principal Foods:

  a. The chief food is the shoots and buds of conifers, for which reason it is disliked by the Forestry Commission.

  b. It will also eat blaeberries, raspberries, corn of any kind, bracken and insects. It is in fact practically omnivorous, like blackgame.

vii. Flight:

  a. Can gain speed and height with remarkable rapidity and deceptive ease.

  b. May take off from a tree branch with a crackling of broken twigs, but a notable feature of its flight is generally the silence.

viii. Methods of shooting:

  a. Almost invariably driven. This is the only satisfactory way of shooting them.

  b. It may be possible to get between them and their feeding grounds when outside the woods eating, say, stooks of oats, but they are usually too cunning to allow anyone to walk within range.

ix. Points to note when shooting:

  a. Range is usually easier to estimate than with blackgame because almost invariably within sight of trees when shooting. Still easy to take shots out of range because of size.

  b. Slow wing beat is deceptive as liable to be moving very fast. Therefore fast swing required.

  c. When shot they can usually be heard crashing through the branches of the trees.

d. When young sometimes encountered on the edge of moor and forest and it is possible at first glance to mistake them for a pheasant, except for square tail.

e. No. 5s or No. 4s are advisable when shooting 'capper' and remember the range of the gun.

Section 5. *The Grey, or Common Partridge*

Perdix perdix is well known to almost everyone.

i. Habitat and Distribution: The habitat is generally agricultural or grass land, but it is also found on moors and sandy soil almost everywhere in the British Isles, except very high ground.

ii. Seasons:

a. Shooting, or Open, Season from 1st September to 1st February inclusive.

b. Breeding, or Close, Season from 2nd February to 31st August inclusive.

iii. Average Appearance, Markings and Size (Male and Female):

a. A grey-brown bird with rufous crown of head and short rufous tail. Short winged.

b. Chestnut horseshoe on breast usually more marked on male, but not infallible difference. Hen usually greyer about head.

c. Hen has narrow wavy crossbar of buff on wing coverts, cock has chestnut and dark blotches.

d. Average size about 12 inches from tip of beak to tail and weight about 13–15 oz.; hen about 12 oz.

iv. Call: A penetrating 'chissick' sound to attract and warn others. Both assembly and warning call before flight.

v. Breeding Habits:

a. Will pair as early as December/January, but may re-form coveys or pack again if weather subsequently severe.

b. Pairs devoted to each other and will often try out several sites for nest before making final choice.

c. Nest is merely scrape filled with grass and may be in exposed situation, near human habitation, or rough ground close to busy road, etc.

d. The number of eggs laid may vary from 10–20. Two birds have been known to lay in same nest.

    e. Incubation usually starts about the middle of May and lasts about 22–25 days.

vi. Principal Foods:

    a. A fairly wide range of insects, worms, slugs and similar live food.

    b. Also comparatively wide range of vegetable food varying from grain, weed and grass seeds, clover, cabbage and even heather shoots, blaeberry, etc. Depending on habitat.

vii. Diseases to which notably susceptible:

    a. Coccidiosis. As with the red grouse, chiefly common amongst chicks.

    b. Pneumonia, when chicks unduly wet and cold and unable to get dry due to weather conditions.

    c. Trichostrongylus tenuis: a similar but more minute parasitic worm to that infecting grouse. Has similar life cycle to *T. gracilis* and passes through droppings to plants and so back to partridge. N.B.: Therefore the larger the stock the greater the possibility of infection.

viii. Flight:

    a. Usually only for short distances of 200–300 yards flighting to 'jugging' ground to roost at night, or to feeding grounds soon after dawn, unless disturbed.

    b. Even when disturbed flight is usually comparatively short, not much more than 400–500 yards.

ix. Packing:

    a. Partridges will not normally leave the covey unless it is split up by shooting, until pairing starts.

    b. If the coveys have been much driven and shot at they are liable to join together and form packs of 50–100 or more, but seldom as large as grouse packs.

    c. Packing is also sometimes noted at breeding time when a form of 'lek' may be seen where partridges are plentiful. 'Chissicking' is very loud and noticeable feature.

    d. Even when packing partridges seem to split up into individual coveys to 'jug' at night. N.B.: Usually jug facing outwards so that ring of droppings may be seen and num-

bers of birds counted accordingly. Paired birds jug and sit
head to tail for all-round watch.

x. Migration:

   a. Partridges do undoubtedly occasionally leave their ground
for one reason or another. May very occasionally be seen at
unusual height in covey obviously bound on longish flight.

   b. Reasons may be:
Exceptional weather conditions. Stocks have been observed
actually blown off ground in high winds and failed to return.
Have also been observed to leave during heavy snow: i.e.
driven by hunger.
Undue persecution, harrying by man or other predators
might also cause stock to leave (N.B.: Kite-hawk).
Lack of suitable food, i.e. chemical farming methods killing
insect life might also drive stock away.

   c. Such migration to more suitable feeding grounds might of
course be purely temporary. Fields of laid corn will attract
game from a surprising distance, for instance.

   d. Distances of 8–10 miles have been recorded and 3–4 are
probably common, but there is reason to consider that
much greater distances may sometimes be covered.

   e. In general, however, wild partridges are less likely to stray
than most game birds.

xi. Rearing:

   a. Eggs under broodies, or in incubators: day old chicks with
bantams or brooder units: Possibly not as easy as redlegs.

   b. Unless put out in pens of about a dozen or so around the
shoot and released by degrees to establish 'coveys' they are
inclined to pack.

xii. Methods of shooting:

   a. Walking-up is one of the commoner ways of shooting
partridges where beaters are not available.

   b. Driven partridge shooting is widely practised in East
Anglia, Hampshire and parts of other southern counties,
but on downland very different to East Anglian birds.

   c. Dogging over pointers, once common in muzzle-loading
days is now much rarer, but has the advantage, not always

realised by those who have not done it, that old barren stock can be picked off and the coveys split up early to improve the shooting.

xiii. Points to note when shooting:

- *a.* The whir of wings of a rising covey is very different from the silent flight of grouse, and the beginner can be very easily over-excited by this sound.
- *b.* A covey usually rises old birds first and then the youngsters. As with grouse, it is important that the beginner picks his birds and does not 'brown' the covey.
- *c.* When shooting driven birds over 20-foot Norfolk hedges the covey is liable to 'explode' at the sight of the guns waiting 30 yards the other side of the hedge.
- *d.* Each bird is then liable to be swerving and curling. Due allowance must be made for the curl.
- *e.* When shooting birds in downland the high birds may be very hard to judge as there are no trees to assist in estimating height and range.
- *f.* Shooting should not generally start until October when strong on wing; 'cheepers' or young birds not full grown should be left, but if very young not likely to survive.
- *g.* The only shooting often advisable in September is old and barren stock over dogs, but in general should not be shot while corn still standing.
- *h.* The usual principle of driving, walking-up, or dogging, is to move the birds towards a suitable holding field, or cover such as roots or kale. As many coveys as possible may be pushed into it and then walked or driven or dogged.
- *i.* To increase sport it is advisable to try to split the coveys up and thus obtain individual shots.

Section 6. *The Red-legged Partridge*

Alectoris rufa is not a native of this country but a successful introduction dating back to the seventeenth century, introduced by Charles II in Windsor and Richmond Parks.

i. Habitat and Distribution: The habitat is similar to that of the grey partridge, but is uncommon north of Yorkshire, though widespread in East Anglia and the southern counties.

Fig. 43. Swinging through the inside wing of a curling bird

ii. Seasons: As for grey partridge.

iii. Average Appearance, Markings and Size (Male and Female):

  a. At distance easily confused with grey partridge.

  b. Red bill and legs, also grey crown and white eye stripe, as well as white throat patch.

  c. Cocks distinguishable by small spur knob on legs, which can be felt in young, if not visible.

  d. Average size rather larger than grey partridge, about $13\frac{1}{2}$ inches from tip of beak to tail and weight 16–18 oz. Hen slightly smaller.

iv. Call: different from grey partridge; harsher deliberate 'chuk-chuk'; sometimes calls when flushed.

v. Breeding Habits:

  a. For years regarded as quarrelsome and the cause of driving grey partridges off their nests. Prejudice now largely disproved and they are widely reared and released.

  b. Times of matings and habits similar to grey partridge, BUT

  c. Noted for interesting fact that both cock and hen can incubate a clutch.

  d. Although numbers in each nest tend to be smaller the overall numbers probably similar to grey partridge.

vi. Principal Foods: As with grey partridge.

vii. Diseases to which notably susceptible: As with grey partridge.

viii. Flight:

  a. Less inclined to take to flight than grey partridge, will run greater distances and probably faster than grey, BUT

  b. When the red-legged does fly he flies fast and boldly and usually for greater distance.

  c. Less inclined to rise in a covey, but more likely to rise singly, thus providing more shooting.

  d. In East Anglia notably inclined to become clogged in wings and feet with running over muddy fields and unable to fly. N.B.: Has been known to take shelter in rabbit holes and drains in this condition.

ix. Packing:

  a. Red-legs are probably less inclined to pack, but

  b. May join packs of grey, as above.

x. Migration:

    a. As with the grey partridge, but

    b. Long-distance migrations probably more common.

xi. Methods of shooting: As with grey partridge, but:

    a. Walking-up is liable to be difficult unless the bird is out-manoeuvred, since it tends to run ahead.

    b. When driven may provide considerable sport due to habit of rising singly.

    c. Contrary to belief can also provide most interesting sport dogging, but, as with walking-up, a question of out-manoeuvring the bird. Only an experienced dog is any use.

xii. Points to note:

    a. Though not popular in the past with gamekeepers and others, there are points in red-leg's favour. It is probably hardier and able to survive on more difficult ground than grey partridge. It is also more easily reared.

    b. It has been suggested that it drives grey partridge off the ground, but observations appear to show that the ·grey is the more quarrelsome bird.

    c. As with grey, will jug in circle. May also sit when paired head to tail.

    d. Though possibly providing good sport, it is not as good a bird from the point of view of the pot. Whether this is largely a matter of cooking is perhaps questionable.

    e. Will often perch in trees or bushes.

Section 7. The Common Pheasant

Phasianus colchicus was not originally a native of this country; was probably brought over by the Romans.

i. Habitat and Distribution: The pheasant, like the grey partridge, is to be found almost everywhere in the British Isles except barren moors and very high ground. Unlike the partridge it favours marshy ground, being in origin a marsh bird.

ii. Seasons:

    a. Shooting, or Open, Season; from 1st October to 1st February inclusive.

L

    b. Breeding, or Close, Season; from 2nd February to 30th September inclusive.

iii. Average Appearance, Markings and Size (Male and Female):

    a. Male highly coloured with glossy dark green head; plumage highly variable due to very many crosses with other varieties, but usually has white ring round neck. Long tail.

    b. Female is more quietly marked, grey-brown mottled markings with shorter tail.

    c. Average size of male about 30–35 inches from tip of beak to tail and weight about 3 lb. Female 21–25 inches; weight about 2½ lb.

    d. It should be noted that there are many different varieties of pheasant, with very many variations on the above. N.B.: Particularly, the melanistic mutant: both cock and hen extremely dark birds; soles of feet pale yellow.

iv. Call: A strident crowing 'Cock-up, cock-up', perhaps best known of all game bird sounds. Will call, or crow, thus:

    a. When going up to roost.

    b. When alarmed. Will often fly off with sustained alarm call in flight. Can be most upsetting to beginner.

    c. In answer to another call, on hearing gunshot, or loud noises, such as church bells.

    d. Call is frequently accompanied by wing beating display in mating season, known as 'drumming'.

v. Breeding habits:

    a. Polygamous: performs a display dance in front of hens involving 'drumming'. May also involve fighting cocks with similar ideas. Hence too many cocks left at end of season undesirable. Hens get no peace.

    b. Mating takes place generally March–April, but may vary greatly with part of country.

    c. Nest may be almost anywhere, usually a hollow scrape in the ground, lined with grass, but they have been known to nest in trees, in abandoned nests and other unlikely places.

    d. The number of eggs may vary from around 8–16 or even more. Occasionally been known to lay in partridge nests. Or in another pheasant nest.

e. Incubation varies starting early April–May and lasting from 23–27 days.

vi. Principal Foods:

a. Even more omnivorous than the partridge, pheasants display a catholic taste in vegetable and insect or animal foods, depending chiefly on their environment.

b. Known foods vary from slugs, snails, worms, field mice, lizards, to wireworms, leatherjackets, etc.; also hazel nuts, beech mast, most berries and all grains, and so on.

c. When present on agricultural land in artificial numbers it is therefore important that they be fed by those who are responsible for them, or compensation paid for damage.

vii. Diseases to which notably susceptible:

a. Coccidiosis: As already noted, a parasitic infection causing acute diarrhoea amongst chicks.

b. Gapes: The gape worm infests the lungs and windpipes of young chicks; is curable, but. can cause many deaths. Similar cycle of infection to strongylus.

c. Pneumonia, as with partridges, when chicks unduly wet and chilled in prolonged rain and wet conditions.

viii. Flight:

a. Cocks particularly liable to fly straight upwards, especially in woods, to clear tops of trees, in manner most disconcerting to beginner.

b. Hens may act as above or slip cunningly over nearest available cover, being much more disinclined to fly or preferring to fly low to ground if possible.

c. After gaining height the pheasant may alter the angle of flight slightly downwards and set its wings. The pace will, if anything, increase and this can make the judgment of an oncoming high shot difficult, especially if there is a cross wind and drift.

ix. Reared and Wild Birds:

a. The very considerable distinction must be fully understood. The wild bird is often judged by the hand-reared animal and there is no similarity beyond looks.

b. The hen pheasant is often termed a bad mother and otherwise maligned, when in fact the bird is merely a hand-reared bird without experience of the wild as taught by an experienced wild hen pheasant mother.

c. A hen pheasant of three or four generations' wild background is a very different animal and not at all a bad mother. She will defend her chicks and rear them well.

d. To some extent the same holds good of the cocks. A cock of several generations' wild upbringing will stay by his hens and his broods and warn of the presence of intruders. He will lead the nye and stand guard.

e. The wilder the bird the more probably it is accustomed to search for its own food and not rely on man. It is therefore probably more liable to stray, or cover ground.

f. The hand-reared pheasant accustomed to being fed and knowing only its home coverts is less likely to stray.

g. A wild mountain or moorland pheasant may cohabit and mate with capercaillie or blackgame. He is truly wild.

x. Straying:

a. Pheasants may in practice move considerable distances, but since most of their movement is on foot this cannot be compared with the migrations of grouse, or to a lesser extent of partridges.

b. It is a matter none the less of some miles, and even a hand-reared pheasant may be found some miles from its home coverts. 8–10 miles is well known. Considerably greater distances are probably covered.

c. Reasons may be:
Uncongenial surroundings, or greater attractions on a neighbouring piece of ground in the shape of cover or of feeding.
Exceptional weather conditions, i.e. prolonged winds and rains from one particular direction to which the coverts are exposed.
Undue persecution or disturbance of the coverts by man or other predators. A systematic poaching raid can clear a covert by frightening birds as much as killing them.
The removal of cover, such as chopping down a wood, or

GAME** 165

clearing undergrowth, or even lifting a crop of kale, may cause birds to stray elsewhere.

Some breeds of pheasants are particularly bad for straying. Reeves are supposedly bad and melanistic mutants have a bad name for this.

Straying may be purely a temporary affair, merely moving over a boundary, or it may be permanent.

xi. Methods of shooting:

a. Walking up is usually only practised in default of beaters, on bye-days, on the roughshoot, or very early in the season round the outlying boundaries or to see stock.

b. Shooting pheasants driven is really the only satisfactory way of shooting them. The whole pleasure of shooting pheasants lies in their presentation to the guns.

c. The one exception to this is the matter of dogging, when old and wily cocks, or wild pheasants, are involved. This can be a very sporting encounter between a wily cock pheasant and an experienced dog, ending in a tricky snap shot at a disappearing rocketer, possibly down a mountainside.

d. Where birds are hand reared on any scale the only possible way to shoot them is driven over the guns in the manner most calculated to present difficult shooting.

xii. Points to note when shooting:

a. Driven pheasant shooting is only likely to start in November when the leaf is fully off the trees.

b. Late hatched birds in any case are seldom mature before the middle of October, though birds not mature enough by then will seldom last the winter.

c. Do not be put off by the close-at-hand cry of a startled cock rising sharply almost beneath the feet. Let it get to a suitable range and then shoot.

d. Do not be hypnotised by that streaming tail of the cock pheasant. Swing right through and shoot on the beak and shoot instinctively. Do not pause to think about it.

e. Remember that the pheasant gliding on set wings is moving as fast as, if not faster than, the bird still vigorously wing beating.

Fig. 44. Swing Right Through. Note second gun with cheek off stock.
Bird only tailed

f. Remember also that the bird on set wings is probably flighting downwards at an angle, often the bird with wings beating is rising deceptively. This may make a considerable difference to the angle of the shot.

g. If there is a strong cross wind blowing a pheasant may have a most deceptive drift or curl in its flight and due allowance must be made for this.

h. A pheasant will seldom if ever fly against the wind, but rising against a strong wind he is likely to have a very considerable curl in flight when flushed.

i. The pheasant coming over the guns will seldom change direction, but he may start climbing quite steeply. The sight of water, even a small stream, may also set him climbing sharply.

j. When the approaching bird climbs sharply the outline changes and the full length of the tail is then seen. Due allowance must be made upwards, swinging straight up through the tail and beak before pulling the trigger, but instinctively. A pause for thought will mean a miss.

Section 8. *The Woodcock*

Scolopax rusticola is a bird known to every game shot, but calculated to cause even the experienced shot a momentary excitement.

i. Habitat and Distribution: Boggy patches in woods are preferred and they are not likely to be found above a certain level, but otherwise their habitat is likely to be anywhere in Great Britain.

ii. Seasons:

    a. Shooting, or Open, Season in England and Wales: 1st October to 31st January inclusive. In Scotland, 1st September to 31st January inclusive.

    b. Breeding, or Close, Season in England and Wales: 1st February to 31st August. In Scotland, 1st February to 30th September inclusive.

iii. Average Appearance, Markings and Size (Male and Female):

    a. Appears to be two distinct types of plumage. One grey in general and the other rufous brown in general. Both achieve perfect dead leaves camouflage.

    b. Prominent eyes set well back in rounded head. Wings round and bill long. No difference between the sexes in plumage.

    c. Average size about 13½ inches from beak to tail. Weight about 8–14 oz.

iv. Call: During display, or 'roding' flights male may make soft croaking call.

v. Breeding Habits:

    a. Mates early, December–January.

    b. Nests equally early; a scrape in the ground amongst the leaves which form a natural camouflage. Usually 3–4 eggs.

    c. Incubation is from 22–25 days, usually during March–April.

    d. Male woodcock traverse a set route in the evenings known as 'roding' flights. They will then mate with any females in their territory. Roding flights are also probably executed by young birds in the spring.

vi. Principal Foods:

    a. Particularly fond of worms for which their bill is so well adapted—3 inches in length and soft upper mandible has sensitive down-curving hook. Feeds by 'dibbling' with this hook.

    b. Also eats larvae, insects, grubs, seeds and grass.

vii. Flight:

    a. Apart from roding flights is usually erratic, darting and zig-zag flight between trees and obstacles.

    b. The woodcock can fly extremely high, but is usually content to remain fairly low down, except when travelling any distance during lengthy nocturnal flights.

    c. Out in the open its flight may be straight and almost laboured and quite slow: an easy shot.

    d. With wind behind it at tree-top level and curling it can defeat the best of shots.

viii. Migration:

    a. Though there is a considerable resident population of woodcock in the country each year, there are also a series of migrations from the Continent which increases the numbers of birds very markedly.

b. These migrating birds arrive on the south and east coast-lines and are frequently exhausted.

c. When recovered they travel inland and so on to Ireland, but are sometimes too exhausted by the journey and die.

d. The cry 'The cock are in' signals their arrival. They can then usually be found in places favoured each year.

e. These migrations are regular annual affairs and there are generally several of them, usually in November–December. Sometimes also known as a 'fall' of cock, indicating their customary exhausted state.

ix. Methods of shooting:

a. Woodcock may be walked-up and may always be encountered when doing so, often in quite unlikely circumstances.

b. They may also be driven when the woodcock are known to be 'in'. Then certain woods are always worth beating in the right part of the country.

c. In Cornwall and certain other parts of the country there are shoots famous for their woodcock.

d. Dogging for woodcock can also be good sport when they are known to be 'in'. At one time done with teams of spaniels, but quite as much fun over one or two well-trained dogs.

x. Points to note:

a. Woodcock have been observed to carry their young, by many reputable observers from St John in the early nineteenth century onwards. Being nocturnal are not easy to observe normally.

b. Their flight when luring a stranger from their young is most peculiar and might well be mistaken for a bird carrying something between its thighs.

c. The tail is tucked down, the head itself and bill are thrust between the thighs and the bird for a short laboured flight is thus flying virtually standing on its head.

d. A chick could be carried thus between the bill and the body and this is no doubt how the woodcock accomplishes the feat.

e. When shot a woodcock should have the sinews of the legs drawn by breaking at the joint and the sinews pulled out at

once. This is reputed to improve the flavour of the woodcock's thigh.

f. The pin feathers, found near the angle of the wings at the
base of the first primaries, are much prized and were once
sought after by miniature painters as useful brushes.

g. Never be tempted to take a careless shot because of the
cry 'Cock over'. Flying at head height amidst trees in zigzag flight, it is easy for the beginner to take an excitable
and dangerous shot. Don't do it.

Section 9. The Snipe

The Common Snipe, the Great Snipe and the Jack Snipe—
Capella gallinago, Capella media and *Lymnocryptes minimus* as they
are known—are the three species of snipe which may be seen,
though the Great, or Double, or Woodcock Snipe is seldom
encountered.

i. Differences and Identification:
Very clear from comparative sizes, but the number of tail
feathers also different.

a. Great Snipe has sixteen tail feathers; mostly white tips.

b. Common, or full, snipe has fourteen, only outside two
being white tipped.

c. Jack, or half, snipe has only twelve tail feathers, which
are pointed.

ii. Habitat and Distribution:
The common snipe breeds throughout Great Britain and is
found almost anywhere boggy or moist conditions are present.
The jack snipe is a common migrant breeding on the Continent. The great snipe is a rare migrant.

iii. Seasons:

a. Shooting, or Open, Season from 12th August to 31st
January inclusive.

b. Breeding, or Close, Season from 1st February to 11th
August inclusive.

N.B.: The great snipe and jack snipe are now protected in
Great Britain but may be shot in Eire.

iv. Average Appearance, Markings and Size (Male and Female):

a. Common snipe: Black and rufous, striped with buff on

back; tail shows white at edges, but not so conspicuously as
great snipe.

b. Great snipe is more size of woodcock, heavier and darker
than the common snipe, also shows white tail feathers.

c. The jack snipe is notable by its much smaller size.

d. The common snipe is about $10\frac{1}{2}$ inches from the bill to
the tip of the tail. Weighs about 6 oz. Great snipe about
11 inches and weighs about 8 oz. Jack snipe about $7\frac{1}{2}$ inches
and weighs about $3\frac{1}{2}$ oz. The sexes are indistinguishable,
but the female is the larger.

v. Call: The common snipe makes a sound resembling quickly
torn cloth, often described as a dry 'Scaap', when flushed.
Common and jack snipe are notable for a 'drumming' or
bleating sound, reputedly made by the outer tail feathers,
during the breeding season, but liable to be made at any time
of the year. The sound is a little like a kid bleating, hence they
are often known as the 'Bog-bleater' or 'Heather-bleater'.
The great snipe makes only an occasional croak.

vi. Breeding habits:

a. Will pair usually in January.

b. Nests usually also early; a hollow in ground, often among
rushes; four is usual number of eggs.

c. Incubation is around 22 days probably during March–
April.

d. Drumming flights are probably most common during the
breeding season.

vii. Principal Foods:
Very much as woodcock.

viii. Flight:

a. Characteristic flight of common snipe is zigzag towering,
or rapidly rising flight.

b. Great snipe and jack snipe more straightforward and
slower flight, though jack may zigzag a little.

c. Jack liable to drop suddenly as though shot after a short
flight, but will rise unharmed.

ix. Migration:

a. Even common snipe breeding here are really only likely
to be transient. All are really migratory birds.

b. To a very considerable extent their movements are dictated by the weather, i.e. hard freezing of their favourite feeding grounds will make them move and high winds will affect them also.

c. Wisps of common snipe are likely to be found each year at similar times in the same feeding grounds.

d. Certain places may be taken, as with woodcock, as annual or periodical snipe grounds suitable for snipe shooting.

x. Methods of shooting:

a. Snipe may be walked up and this is often advocated as the most suitable way of shooting snipe.

b. Some people advocate walking snipe down-wind, maintaining that the bird sits tight and has to get up into the wind to rise and at that instant is easily shot, before it starts its zigzag flight.

c. This may be perfectly true, but it must be remembered that this requires snap shooting and may suit some people and not others. When birds are wild, is not sound.

d. Other people advocate walking up-wind, probably over dogs though not necessarily. The birds may then be approached closer and shot at reasonable range.

e. Driven snipe, if there are sufficient quantities on the ground to warrant driving, can provide very good sport. It is preferable to drive small areas at a time.

f. Dogging snipe requires a good water dog and one with a tender mouth and good nose.

g. A great snipe is very seldom encountered, but usually for all snipe the most suitable cartridges are No. 7s. This does not preclude use of even No. 5s in a well-choked gun at longish range. One such pellet will certainly be enough for such a small bird. This is a matter of confidence in gun and pattern, as well as ability to hold the gun straight.

Section 10. *The Wild Duck*

Anas platyrhynchos, or the Mallard, is well known to every game shot and may be included in the bag during almost any shooting day.

i. Habitat and Distribution: Almost any water anywhere in Great Britain, inland or by the sea shore.

ii. Seasons:

   a. Shooting, or Open, Season in areas below high-water mark of spring tides, 1st September to 20th February inclusive. Inland, 1st September to 31st January inclusive.

   b. Breeding, or Close, Season in areas below high-water mark of spring tides, 21st February to 31st August inclusive. Inland, 1st February to 31st August inclusive.

iii. Average Appearance, Markings and Size (Male and Female):

   a. Male has glossy green head, white collar and purplish brown breast, pale grey underparts, yellowish bill.

   b. Female is mottled brown with greenish bill and orange legs. Both well known.

   c. Average size 23 inches from tip of beak to tail and weight about $2\frac{1}{2}$ lb to $2\frac{3}{4}$ lb. Female slightly less.

iv. Call: Well-known 'Quark'; varying from alarm calls to feeding calls and not to be confused.

v. Breeding Habits:

   a. Pairs January–February and is monogamous.

   b. Nests from February onwards, but probably March–April, depending on location and weather conditions.

   c. Nests may be quite large affairs, lined with down, grass and reeds. Usually close to water, but may be a very considerable distance away; though usually with access. May even be up trees in deserted nests of other birds.

   d. Number of eggs averages from 8 to 10.

   e. Incubation period is from 27–29 days.

vi. Principal Foods:

   a. Surface feeders which feed by 'dabbling', or up-ending and feeding on weeds, grubs, grit, etc.

   b. Also feed on any grain, rotted potatoes, young grass and similar food inland.

vii. Flight:

   a. Rising flight is liable to be deceptively fast and due allowance should be made for upwards swing, well above.

   b. Flighting in to decoys at a flight pond, precisely the reverse is the case, as descent with 'paddles' down is deceptively fast. Requires swing well through below.

   c. When flushed will frequently circle round over the position from which just departed.

   d. Flight is usually swift and at fair height.

viii. Movement:

   a. May be over a very wide area relating to weather, storms at sea, freezing of inland waters, high winds, etc.

   b. Also migratory, and presence of migrating birds may temporarily swell numbers.

   c. Hand-reared mallard tend to return to the pond on which they were reared.

   d. May join with wild birds and migrate when fully grown and after experience of shooting.

ix. Methods of Shooting and Points to Note:

   a. Walking-up may be practised in boggy ground, but usually only by a limited number of guns.

   b. Driving may be possible on a limited scale and driven mallard certainly provide high and spectacular shooting, but not practical on any scale.

   c. Dogging is seldom practical except on boggy ground where the duck are sitting tight after a very cold snap, or in high wind.

   d. A dog is however generally necessary whenever shooting duck and must be a good water dog.

   e. One of the commoner ways of shooting mallard inland is on a flight pond at the evening flight, over decoys.

   f. The number of guns on any decoy pond must be strictly limited.

   g. The guns must always allow the duck to come well in before shooting.

   h. In eclipse the drake is hardly recognisable, i.e. during breeding season, when much resembles duck. Regains full plumage about October.

x. Other types of Wild Duck liable to be encountered:

   a. Teal. Smallest of all ducks. Flight very rapid, usually in flocks; usually low and flight can be erratic. Rises particularly fast, known as springing. Average 14 inches tip of beak to tail. Weight about 11–13 oz.

b. Wigeon. More likely found on coast except in Scotland. Average 18 inches from tip of beak to tail. Chestnut head, grey body, distinctive white belly. Flights in compact flocks; rafts often rest at sea. Distinctive high whistling call. May be met inland when flighting, or when weather very wild and stormy at sea.

Section 11. *Ground game*

Hares and Rabbits are classified collectively as Lagomorpha of the Leporidae family; notable in Great Britain as follows:

HARES

i. Habitat and Distribution:

a. *Lepus Europaeus*, or the common brown hare, is to be found almost anywhere in the country below a certain level except in highly populated areas, but patchy distribution.

b. *Lepus timidus Scoticus* and his cousin *Lepus timidus Hibernicus*, or the blue mountain hares of Scotland and Ireland, are very similar, each in their respective areas found on moorland above their common brown relation.

ii. Seasons: There is no close season for hares, but they may not be offered for sale between the months of March and July inclusive. On moorland and unenclosed lands hares may be shot by the occupier and persons authorised by him between 11th December and 31st March only. In Scotland between 1st July and 31st March.

iii. Differences between brown and blue hares:

a. Brown hare heavier and generally much larger, though own size varies considerably with district between 6–12 lb.

b. Blue hare lighter boned, bluish colouring when young, adult grey turns white in winter, weighs generally between 5–7 lb.

c. Brown hare seldom 'goes to ground', but this is a common practice of blue hare.

d. Litters of brown hare vary from 2–5, but blue hare may have up to 8. Young of both termed leverets.

iv. Breeding Habits:
- *a.* Will breed throughout the year depending to a very large extent on the weather. Double oestrus or second fertilisation is not uncommon.
- *b.* Generally breeding madness affects hares in March, when the bucks are to be seen fighting and all playing follow-my-leader in considerable numbers.
- *c.* Although polygamous, the buck probably has more contact with does than is generally suspected.
- *d.* Young are born fully furred in the 'form' or scrape in which doe lies.
- *e.* At very early age are carried to separate forms and fed in rotation by doe.

v. Points to note:
- *a.* Principal foods may include any grasses or herbage and roots.
- *b.* It appears almost certain that in some areas hares do from time to time migrate considerable distances. Reasons for this may be weather, mating instinct, choice of foods available, undue persecution, etc.
- *c.* Hares are not subject to myxomatosis, but in very wet conditions may contract liver disease and waste away.
- *d.* Considerable numbers must be annually killed on roads and by rollers and due to modern farming practices.

vi. Methods of shooting:
- *a.* Walking-up. One well-tried method, very commonly practised.
- *b.* Driving. Usually in combination with walking-up at back-end hare drives.
- *c.* Dogging. Over dogs at any time of year, but dogs should be steady to fur.

RABBITS
i. Habitat and Distribution: *Oryctolagus cuniculus cuniculus*, in spite of myxomatosis, is to be found in almost every county in the British Isles in increasing quantities.
ii. Seasons: There is no close season for rabbits. They are classified as vermin and may be shot throughout the year.

iii. Breeding Habits:

    a. Will breed throughout the year and regardless of the weather. Have amazing ability to recover from diseases and epidemics which reduce numbers, e.g. myxomatosis.

    b. Generally digs short hole, or 'stop', and doe kindles there. Young are born blind and helpless.

    c. Litters may vary from as little as two to eleven and double oestrus, or second fertilisation, is not exceptional.

    d. Gestation period six weeks and young unable to look after themselves for some three weeks.

iv. Points to note:

    a. Size of the rabbit is likely to be governed by the feeding available. Normally between 2–3 lb.

    b. Bucks can fight fiercely with each other disputing territory. Have shorter, thicker heads than does.

    c. Equipped as burrowing animal, but 'scrub' rabbits which live in the open are also common. Lie in form like hare.

    d. Rabbit lying out usually owes survival to ability to remain 'clapped' down, escaping observation, but also clever at dodging in cover.

    e. Rabbit only capable of short burst of speed in the open. Can be run down by man.

v. Methods of shooting:

    a. Walking-up common, but usually desirable to stink out holes beforehand to make sure rabbits are lying out. Then good sport can be had.

    b. Driven. Less common today; important when rabbits are being driven to stand with back to the direction of the drive and take them behind as they run past.

    c. Dogging. Can be good sport bustling them out of cover with dogs and, like most rabbit shooting, affords snap shooting of some difficulty as rabbit twists and turns.

    d. Care must always be had of dogs and other guns and beaters when shooting any ground game, but especially rabbits.

vi. Ferreting:

    a. Though strictly speaking an interest outside game shooting, the game shot should have a knowledge of ferreting and will

M

find it can provide amusing and sometimes extremely interesting out-of-season sport.

b. Two distinct types of ferret: large white creamy type, or smaller dark brown polecat-ferret cross, usually known as fitchet.

c. Male known as hob, female as jill. May have two litters a year of from 6–10. Sexes should be segregated if many kept.

d. Best handled as often as possible and kept clean and in good draught-free hutch. Should be tame and not ready to bite any hand near them.

e. Carried in travelling box slung over shoulder. Should also contain collars, bells and knotted line and muzzles if used, but best to use without encumbrance.

f. Once the ferret has been inserted in likely burrow care must be taken to stand above and clear, not showing, or rabbits will not bolt.

g. Dogs and guns must be accustomed to sudden appearance of ferret and not mistake for rabbit.

h. Line ferret may have to be used when 'lie up' occurs and digging needed to locate ferret in hole.

i. ·410 or cartridge adaptors are useful here as snap shooting involved at close range and otherwise rabbit may be shot to pieces.

GENERAL NOTES

i. Rabbits should always be paunched, i.e. gutted, after being shot.

ii. If the tip of a knife is inserted in the lower belly and ripped up to the ribs the entire guts can be turned out with a twist of the wrist. A finger hooked behind the stomach will remove them, if sticking.

iii. Hares should never be paunched but should be left entire. When properly shot well forward they are best hung head upwards to avoid loss of the blood for use in soup.

iv. To avoid blow flies in hot weather the application of pepper to heads and backsides is recommended in both hares and rabbits.

v. Both hares and rabbits may be hocked and legged, i.e.:

a. Legged by slitting hind leg and thrusting other through for carrying. Two may thus be paired.

    b. Hocked, when hind tendon is nicked after legging to prevent the legs slipping apart.

vi. All ground game is liable to be pegged by hunting dogs when lying clapped down, i.e. seized before it can break away and run.

vii. Snares for rabbits or hares should never be allowed on fences, as too often other game using the run worn in the grass by the ground game will be caught instead.

Section 12. *Woodpigeon and Various*

Columba palumbus, although rated as a pest, can also provide as good and interesting shooting as any game bird at times, with the advantage that it may be shot throughout the year.

i. Breeding habits and appearance:

    a. The average woodpigeon pair have five clutches a year.

    b. Each clutch consists of two eggs and the incubation period is eighteen days.

    c. Fortunately it is estimated that only about one pair of squabs reach full maturity, since they have many enemies other than man.

    d. The young gain their familiar neck ring after sixteen weeks.

ii. Movements and feeding:

    a. Though migratory birds from the Continent do appear in sometimes quite considerable numbers, the bulk of the damage in this country is probably due to hungry flocks of home-bred pigeon searching for food.

    b. The collarless 'foreigners' so often seen are merely flocks of juvenile birds, not yet fully marked. They can fly freely and forage on their own within a few weeks and after three months have lost all ties with the parents.

    c. It is considered, however, that the average pigeon movement is probably restricted to a range of about 25 miles from the breeding grounds, though exceptional winds or weather or lack of feeding might lead to a greater area being covered.

    d. The pigeon is an omnivorous and greedy feeder of all greenstuffs, grains, berries and similar vegetable matter. Hence is hated by the farmer.

iii. Methods of shooting:

  a. Shooting may be in organised parties stationed in each wood or cover over a wide area, but this is seldom likely to be very successful, especially should any woods be left unmanned as too often is the case. The birds will inevitably find them.

  b. Woodpigeon may always figure in the bag after any sort of shooting day and may have provided very sporting high shots. They will however often cunningly slip out of a tree on the opposite side to the approaching gun.

  c. The greatest sport can be had shooting them over decoys, when sometimes very considerable numbers running into several hundreds can be shot by the expert who takes time and trouble with his preparations.

iv. Shooting over decoys:

  a. The places where the birds are feeding must be noted as well as discovering what is attracting them. This may involve a lengthy reconnaisance and shooting several birds to examine the contents of their crops. But such preparation is never wasted.

  b. The hide must next be erected with regard to the direction of the wind and line of the pigeon's approach.

  c. It must be close to the place most favoured by the birds, leaving room for uncramped shooting and at the same time well camouflaged from view.

  d. If a suitable ditch and hedge are conveniently placed a billhook and some freshly cut branches should soon provide an effective hide. Otherwise camouflage netting and sticks may be necessary. Straw bales are excellent.

  e. The decoys, at least six in number, preferably dead birds, should be set out realistically propped up facing roughly into the wind and not more than a yard or so apart. A 'lofted' decoy on a tree branch is an asset.

  f. The pigeon shooter must remain still and let the birds come in to the decoys. Movement must be kept to minimum. Dead birds and stray feathers should be removed, but if the birds are really coming in they will not be checked by anything.

g. Very considerable sport may be had from a 'hochsitz' or elevated hide up a tree. Such a platform must be steady, but with decoys suitably lofted on branches nearby this can provide very sporting shooting as the birds come on at all angles over the tree-tops.

v. N.B.: Take great care NOT to shoot racing pigeons by accident. Learn what they look like and leave doubtful birds alone. If one is shot see that the ring is given in to the local police station or nearest fancier.

vi. Golden Plover.

a. In small or large flocks may sometimes come over the guns on a shooting day, light brown birds spotted yellow.
b. Should not be despised if providing a sporting shot.
c. It is often difficult to select birds cleanly out of a large flock, but do not 'brown'.
d. When out of range they will often sweep in closer if a shot is fired, or a shrill whistle blown.

vii. Crows, Magpies, Rooks, Jackdaws, Jays and Grey Squirrels.

a. Any or all of these may figure in the Various column at the end of a shooting day.
b. If there is a price on the head of predators and a kitty for the winner, stoats, weasels, mink, squirrels, rats and foxes may sometimes be included as well.
c. Foxes however should NOT be shot in hunting country and it is always as well to check your host's views on them and other Various beforehand.

PART 3

THE ORGANISATION AND METHOD OF SHOOTING

Section 1. The Preparation for the Shooting Day

This must, of course, vary very considerably from shoot to shoot and shooting to shooting, as well as from day to day:

i. Obviously there can be little comparison between a low-ground pheasant shoot and a dogging moor, or between a many-keepered shoot and a roughshoot, but:

   a. In a very real sense the preparation for any shooting day is the amount of work the keeper, or organiser, has put in during the previous twelve months.

   b. This should never be forgotten when a shooting day has been enjoyed.

ii. In general last-minute preparations and plans for the day's shooting will have been made by the keeper, and/or organiser, on the day previous to the shoot, even though the date and general outline plans may have been decided on months beforehand.

   a. Suitable alternatives will also have been decided on should they be necessary in the event of abrupt changes of wind or weather.

   b. The moorland keeper will have checked the condition of his butts and the low-ground keeper will have seen to it that his pegs were suitably sited for the various stands on each drive.

   c. The number of experienced and inexperienced beaters available will have been considered carefully and discussed along with the question of:

   d. Employment of those with dogs to pick up and where these should be stationed to be of most use.

   e. The employment of those experienced enough as flankers, stops, or loaders where required.

   f. The plans for their transport and that of the guns between drives and the question of alternatives always considered in case required.

  g. Arrangements will have been made for their payment at the current rates and for refreshment if provided.

  h. Arrangements will have been made as to times and place of meeting, moving off, and the day's schedule approximately timed.

iii. On the morning of the shooting day the keeper will generally have been active by dawn.

  a. Then the first assessments of the day can be made from the way the wind is blowing and general weather signs.

  b. The decision as to which of the prepared plans to put into operation may be made then.

  c. It may be advisable to make a quick check round the boundaries of the low-ground shoot as this is a time when two-legged or four-legged foxes may be encountered, and their presence prevented from spoiling a part of the day.

  d. On some shoots it may be advisable to place stops out early to check any leak of birds over a boundary inconveniently placed close to a covert: i.e. an experienced beater is set in a suitable position where by his presence and by occasionally tapping lightly with a stick he prevents the birds from leaving covert.

  e. It may be necessary to set sewelling in place, either with a similar object to *d.* above, or to cause the birds to take to wing at set points, i.e. a long cord with coloured rags attached at 18-inch intervals is staked about 18 inches or 2 feet up from the ground to cover the particular area required. N.B.: It is undesirable to leave sewelling out overnight and is slack practice to do so.

iv. Prior to the arrival of the game shots the beaters, flankers, stops and pickers-up will probably have been assembled, and

  a. If their duties for the day have not already been outlined and the plan for the day explained, this will now be done.

  b. Each will be assigned his place in the line according to age and experience, i.e. the youngest and least experienced nearest the keeper or responsible beater.

    c. Transport will have been checked and arranged and the last-minute plans agreed between keeper and organiser.

    d. It is MOST important that these two at least should fully understand each other and the arrangements for the day. N.B.: Using a large-scale map will avoid most possibilities of misunderstanding.

v. With the arrival of the guests the final preparations for the day should fall into place:

    a. Numbers will either be drawn for, or detailed by the organiser host. Or:

    b. He may prefer to place his guns at each stand with a view to placing the weaker shots between the good ones.

    c. Or he may prefer placing his guns to ensure that each has his fair share of good stands. Often a very difficult task, since birds will seldom oblige by flying where expected.

    d. A briefing should be given by the organiser/host as to the plans for the day so that everyone understands roughly the outline of what to expect.

    e. The more complete the briefing the better, and large-scale maps can be useful to avoid mistakes, e.g. guests waiting with their backs to the driven birds, or lining up in the wrong butts.

    f. In the case of complete strangers to the shoot it is often advisable to see they have someone in attendance, or next to them, who can explain what to expect at each stand.

vi. At the agreed time both beaters and guns should be in their respective positions awaiting the signal to start the day.

Section 2. The Beaters

For a driven day's shooting the beaters are an essential part of the day, but the distinction between driving partridges and grouse and beating pheasants out of covert must be appreciated: The following points may be noted:

i. The more experienced the beater the better, since this is NOT the simple task it might appear and bad beaters can easily wreck a drive or a day.

    a. An experienced beater with an experienced steady dog (N.B.: not necessarily a gun dog; it is merely required to indicate the presence of game, nothing else) is worth any number of inexperienced beaters.

b. But the beater must have his heart in his job. He must also be intelligent. Nothing is worse than the 'pressed' beater, or the beater with a grievance.

ii. The beaters must be under the command of the keeper, or an experienced beater who knows exactly what is required beforehand at each drive:

a. The controller usually takes the centre.

b. He must have control, preferably by whistle or signal, NOT shouting, over the pace and behaviour of the beaters, whether stationed in the centre or on one flank.

c. The line must be kept straight, or at an angle, or in horse-shoe or crescent shape as required to drive the game in the required direction.

d. There should be no shouting, whistling, or yelling from the beaters.

e. The rougher the cover the slower the pace and the more sticks should be kept tapping continuously.

f. Each patch of rough cover should be carefully worked out by the nearest beaters.

g. As each bird or covey rises the line should halt for a moment while the nearest beater makes sure that all the birds have risen from that spot.

iii. The beaters should be equipped with suitable clothing for the circumstances.

a. On the moor, dependent on the weather, shorts and shirt, or wet-weather clothes, but stout walking boots will be required either way. On many moors they will be given flags on six-foot canes which they will hold up as they approach the butts to indicate their presence.

b. On the low-ground shoot, dependent on the ground and the weather, old thornproof garments, or wet weather clothes to withstand wet roots.

c. On some major shoots special protective clothing is provided for the beaters, usually with distinctively marked headgear, so that they can be seen by the guns from a distance.

iv. Shortage of beaters has led to:

    a. The employment of undergraduates, housed in a hostel and paid a flat rate, on some grouse moors.

    b. The employment of female beaters where available. Often keener and more willing than males.

    c. The employment on occasion of one or more handlers with trained dogs in lieu of beaters. N.B.: Teams of spaniels have been used for this, but one or two retrievers or pointer-retrievers can do a very efficient job if trained.

    d. Few people realise that the above can be quite as good as, if not better than, indifferent humans.

    e. The wages of beaters are constantly increasing and at present £10 is about the minimum adult wage a day, with local variations, mostly upwards.

Section 3. *The Flanker*

The task of flanking efficiently is all-important and can make or mar any drive. It is not always fully understood.

i. The flanker should be equipped with a white flag on a cane about six feet long.

    a. He should be stationed on either flank in a position where it is considered from experience likely that the birds may break.

    b. There may be more than one flanker required on either side, but they must be experienced and fully understand their job.

    c. They must work as a team, in line with each other and in accord with the line of beaters. Working intelligently they can actually 'funnel' birds over the guns.

ii. As far as possible the flanker should stay out of sight and watch the approach of the beaters and the movement of the coveys ahead of them:

    a. He may have to take cover in a hedge or ditch, or else in a suitable clump of heather on the moor. Not usually on a knoll, but rather in front of it.

    b. As soon as he sees a covey level with him beginning to break to his side he should jump forward and wave his flag vigorously two or three times before taking cover again. It is then the turn of the flanker beyond him.

    c. If he waves too soon he may turn the covey back over the beaters.

iii. When the beating line is crescent-shaped the flankers at each point of the crescent, or horseshoe, should also carry flags, which must be used with discretion in the same way for the same purpose.

iv. The flanker's job is progressively more difficult as the season passes:

    a. In the early stages it is comparatively simple when the birds have not been driven over the guns.

    b. As the birds grow more experienced and stronger on the wing it is not only more difficult, but more important.

    c. Flanking old or wild birds is a skilled and often quite impossible task.

    d. Later in the season it is often worth reinforcing the flanker with a walking gun if this can be done.

Section 4. *The Stop*

Like the flanker's task, that of the stop is both skilled and all-important in that a stop who is not doing his job properly can easily ruin a drive.

i. All the stop requires is a strong stick and patience.

    a. He should be prepared to stand quietly occasionally tapping with his stick to prevent game from breaking in his direction.

    b. A stop must NOT be noisy; if accompanied by another they should not talk loudly, nor should he attempt to shout to neighbouring stops.

    c. He is not intended to frighten the game and possibly cause it to leave the covert, or run back elsewhere. His job is purely to stop a possible way of escape.

ii. The stop may sometimes be equipped with a length of sewelling.

    a. In addition to a tap with his stick occasionally he may be required to give the sewell line a jerk to keep the rags swinging as a deterrent to game.

    b. He will not be expected to agitate the sewell line unduly.

iii. As indicated, a stop may start early in the day where his presence is required to block a possible leak of birds over a boundary.

iv. As the line of beaters approaches the stop is liable to see and hear evidence of the game.

    a. In many cases he may be reinforced by a gun to take any birds which break at that point.

    b. As far as possible he should restrict himself to tapping with his stick, merely increasing the tempo as the line approaches him. If a bird looks like breaking he may try to check it by waving his arms.

    c. As the line passes his stance he can join them again.

Section 5. The Sewelling

The sewel line has already been described. It is composed of any coloured strips of cloth, or plastic, tied to a length of cord:

i. It is easy enough to make one up, of strips cut from plastic sacks, but they can be bought ready made.

    a. At one time it was possible to buy a harness with a winder for the sewell line on it, which is useful, but

    b. In general they can usually be readily enough rolled up and handled in convenient lengths.

ii. They can be used as stops, or as flushing points.

    a. For effective use a stop is best employed at one end, occasionally jerking the sewelling as indicated.

    b. Though principally used on pheasant coverts, they can be usefully employed in roots when partridge driving as a stop at the end of the drills.

iii. Intelligently used, sewelling can make up for a lack of beaters.

    a. It can also be used effectively to divide coverts and

    b. To enhance the scope and variety of a small shoot.

iv. Sewelling should not be left out overnight.

    a. It loses half its value if the birds learn to grow accustomed to it.

    b. It will lose all traces of smell of humans and this should not be underestimated.

   c. It will grow damp and sodden, again losing half its value.

   d. Even if it means setting it up at dawn, or beforehand, and picking it up the same night, or after use, this should be done.

   e. Hence the convenience of a special harness and winding frame. The sewelling can be laid and picked up quickly by the experienced hand while the shoot is in progress.

v. A beater, or under-keeper, who is skilled in laying a sewel line and is versed in the plans for the day may be a considerable asset, moving ahead and re-laying his line on the next beat.

vi. The use of balloons as a sort of aerial sewel line has been suggested for use on moors, but not so far tried.

Section 6. *The Kite Hawk*

The kite hawk is merely a kite shaped like a hovering hawk which is flown ahead of the walking guns.

i. It is an age-old method of hunting—

   a. Originally used in the gentle art of netting game.

   b. It was also used frequently in the days of muzzle loaders.

ii. Although seldom used today, they are still available in some gunsmiths' lists and are simply enough made, but

   a. They should be used with considerable care.

   b. They will cause coveys which have already grown wild to stay down until pushed up by the dogs; BUT

   c. Used too often they might well cause the game to desert the ground altogether and move elsewhere.

iii. The device obviously has its limitations anyway.

   a. They can only be used on a day which is suitably windy.

   b. They cannot be used in the neighbourhood of trees, power lines or telephone wires.

   c. One person is occupied fully with the job of keeping the kite flying.

iv. In spite of the comments above, this device does have its uses and might be occasionally employed more widely.

   a. Where it is desired to shoot more game for the good of the

shoot, i.e. where there are too many old birds which are
otherwise too wild to approach.

b. As an aid to driving as in *a*. above, when too many birds
have been left on the moor.

Section 7. The Pick-up

The pick-up after a good day's well-organised driven shooting
should be within 1 or 2 per cent of the total shot.

i. It is probably true to say that, except in a very few particularly
well-organised shoots, it is seldom within 25 per cent of the
the total shot.

a. Admittedly some shoots rely on being able to pick up a
percentage of dead and crippled birds on the day after the
shooting but this can disturb game unduly.

b. It is better done on the day, but is seldom likely to be more
than a proportion of the true amount lost to the bag.

ii. Paradoxically, the better the shoot and the better the guns
generally, the more the services of a good team are required
picking-up.

a. Bad shots miss clean. There is no problem of picking-up
after them if the shooting is difficult.

b. Good shots are liable to land a pellet or two in the bird
when there is every excuse for missing; e.g. when birds are
curling deceptively over the line in a high wind.

iii. It is not the birds shot within range of the gun which are
generally lost.

a. A dog handler between two guns can usually account for
most of these.

b. These are mostly consciously marked by the gun, or someone in the line, and duly picked or noted for later search.

iv. Especially, as noted in ii. above, in the better shoots where
high birds come curling over the line at speed birds are liable
to drop a long way back:

a. If possible, without interfering with the subsequent drives,
it is desirable to have at least one picker-up well behind,
some 200–300 yards behind the guns.

    b. Such a picker-up with an experienced dog, or better still pair of dogs, capable of marking well at long range and retrieving dead birds and runners fast in all conditions, is capable of adding to the bag by 20 per cent.

v. Anyone acting as picker-up in such conditions at driven grouse, or partridges, or at high pheasants, cannot fail to be surprised at first by the number of birds which fall dead a quarter of a mile or more behind the line.

    a. He must be adept at marking when a bird has been hit and marking its flight.

    b. In practice, if a bird has been seriously hit it will invariably show it by reactions he can recognise within his range of vision, though possibly well beyond view from the line itself.

    c. Any variations in normal flight or landing are suspect and will bear investigation.

vi. The picker-up may be a professional, either keeper or dog handler, or he may be an amateur.

    a. The shoot which can rely on the services of willing amateurs with good dogs is fortunate.

    b. Really good and experienced hands at picking up with well-trained dogs are in very short supply.

vii. The keen picker-up can have in his own way every bit as interesting sport as the guns and may even contribute more to the bag than some of them.

    a. He can also learn a great deal about shooting by watching others.

    b. He can also learn a great deal about the habits of game.

viii. The amateur picker-up must however regard himself as under the orders of the head keeper:

    a. He should not send his dog to retrieve behind the line until the drive is finished.

    b. He should make sure that he does not send his dog into any ground reserved for the next drive.

    c. He must not lose control of his dog, or shout or whistle noisily during the drive. (Preferably not at any time.)

    d. He should not regard the shoot as an occasion for training his dog.

    e. He should be prepared to join in and beat with the best of them.

    f. He should be prepared to forgo his lunch and to remain out after the others have finished in order to find runners or dead birds he has marked.

ix. Picking up the following day is never likely to be as satisfactory as making a clean sweep on the day of the shoot itself.

    a. Because scent is cold and birds which have been lying out overnight are correspondingly harder to find.

    b. Because in the meantime foxes, crows and other predators have had a chance to get in first.

x. Even if the pick-up has been almost entirely successful, however, it is always worth going out early the following day with a dog and a gun—

    a. To pick off any obvious cripples; or any sick-looking birds unable to fly well.

    b. Runners which may have escaped notice are likely to have rejoined their covey or be out in the open feeding.

    c. Some pricked birds may have stiffened up during the night and be found lying dead.

    d. Such birds should all be added to the bag.

xi. It should be every shooting man's aim to kill cleanly whenever he is shooting, and when he has failed to do so he should spare no effort to find the game he has wounded. It is his duty to do so.

    a. When shooting driven game the shooting man should not consider himself absolved from this duty. He should take as active an interest in the picking up as possible.

    b. When walking-up game it is desirable to pick up all the game shot as far as possible, even if it means holding up the line for some time.

    c. The roughshooter has the advantage that he can spare as long as is required for the pick-up.

    d. In dogging it is a part of the sport to ensure a clean pick-up.

PART 4

SHOOT MANAGEMENT

It must be appreciated that in order to produce reasonable shooting in any circumstances a great deal of work and preparation is involved both in the Close Season and during the Shooting Season itself.

A. *The Moor*

Section 1. Heather Burning

Controlled by The Heather and Grass Burning (England and Wales) Regulations of 1949 and by long series of Acts in Scotland.

i. Generally not allowed between 31st March and November.

    a. Though sometimes practised in the autumn after the shooting has finished, burning is more generally restricted to suitable dry days between January and April.

    b. When the ground is really sodden, burning is hopeless, as when snow is on the ground.

    c. It is also dangerous to burn when there is a high wind, or the fires may get out of control.

    d. The number of days when burning is possible are thus very limited.

ii. Unless the heather is regularly burned the moor will become almost useless for grouse.

iii. Old thick tussocks of heather are not good for grouse:

    a. They provide little real feeding value.

    b. They have none of the fresh green shoots grouse like.

    c. They provide shelter for ticks, which sometimes infest grouse.

iv. Burning is restricted to certain areas each year:

    a. Usually 3–5 acre patches spread over the moor.

    b. In this way the entire moor is burned in rotation over a fifteen-year period.

    c. Known shelter belts or feed belts favoured by the grouse are of course dealt with particularly carefully so that the ensuing season's shooting is not affected.

v. Burning is usually against the wind, to prevent the fire getting out of control;

  a. If the wind changes or rises this can be an important factor.
  b. The burning must also not be allowed to get deep into peaty soil, when it may possibly smoulder for months.
  c. If either of these happens a considerable acreage of the moor may be ruined for a number of years to come.

vi. On some moors as a matter of policy and to save time larger strips of 20 acres or more are burned at one time.

  a. A team of seven or eight experienced burners do well if they burn 40 acres a day.
  b. A burning lamp, a birch besom per man and an experienced team are necessary.

vii. The limiting factors on heather burning therefore are:

  a. Time available for the job when conditions are suitable.
  b. The availability of suitable experienced labour at the right time.
  c. The weather, even when a. and b. above are fulfilled, is the deciding factor.

N.B.: It is suggested that regular burning may remove important elements in the soil which are not subsequently replaced and that this may be an important factor not so far sufficiently examined.

Section 2. Drainage

i. Almost every moor has areas of boggy soil, which would be improved by drainage.

ii. If such areas are extensive effective drainage can make a considerable difference to the number of grouse a moor can carry.

iii. Deep-sided drains must however be provided with occasional breaks to allow young birds to escape, otherwise they can be death traps to chicks of all game species.

Section 3. Heather Beetle and Bracken

i. Heather beetle is a small brownish beetle which attacks the heather and leaves patches which look as if they have been frosted.

ii. The only remedy for this appears to be burning, which destroys the beetle as well.

iii. Bracken is another increasing menace on many moors, where its encroachments are viewed with alarm.

    a. Sprays are available, but a reliable method is to cut the young shoots in May when they first appear.

    b. They must then be cut again the following month when they appear again. This does check spread.

Section 4. Other Annual Tasks on the Moor

i. Repair of tracks across the moor should be undertaken during the close season, preferably in the spring.

    a. Any small drains or bridges should be checked at the same time, for blockages or defects.

    b. The butts should also be carefully inspected and where required improved.

ii. Renewal of grit supplies is important if necessary:

    a. Sharp-edged quartz grit may cost as much as £10 a ton, but it is essential to the health of the grouse.

    b. A ton would probably be required for about 5,000 acres.

iii. Corking of any telephone or fencing wires in places where they may otherwise be death-traps to grouse should not be overlooked. Any new fences should have heather tufts hung on them as a precaution, to prevent the grouse flying into them without seeing them.

Section 5. Butts

i. On some moors perfectly adequate stands may be had in sunken depressions such as provided by a burn, or behind a stone dyke.

ii. Butts may vary considerably between extremes such as:

    a. Merely temporary screens of wire stuffed with heather.

    b. Deep half-sunk stone-built, turf-topped, circular erections likely to last a century or more.

iii. The objection to a circular butt is that it is often easy to lose a sense of direction in the heat of the moment and possibly fire down the line. A straightforward screen, or H-shaped butt, is preferable.

iv. Whatever the type of butt it should be fenced, or else the entrance be capable of being closed.

    a. The object is simply to keep out stray cattle and sheep.

    b. This is largely for the keeper's benefit, since they are easily knocked down as well as being fouled by such intrusions.

v. The butt should be well drained.

    a. There is nothing worse than trying to stand on a slippery mud floor.

    b. Duck boards are probably the best answer if well pegged down, but not if loose and easily capsized.

    c. Otherwise well-drained boards or cement may be the answer.

vi. There must be room for the gun and a loader, if required.

    a. They should be able to stand together with ease.

    b. The better butts provide a shelf, or peg for the cartridge bags, etc. Some even provide a seat for the loader.

    c. Cramped butts are a needless handicap. There must be room to swing easily.

    d. The dog should be left outside. Tied up if not steady.

vii. Some provision should be made for a small man, i.e. turves on the front should be removable so that the height of the butt can be easily adjusted.

    a. Heather turves are usually placed along the top and may be removed to suit the height of the occupant.

    b. He should be able to rest his gun barrels on the edge comfortably by leaning forward slightly.

viii. Lastly, but most important, the butts should be correctly aligned. Butts are sometimes to be found out of line, or at awkward angles to each other, which is simply asking for accidents.

N.B.: The safety markers, one on each side of the butt, to prevent the occupant swinging beyond the safety margins in the heat of the moment, are always worth setting up. A twig set up on end will do quite well. They may save someone's eyesight. They can certainly do no harm.

Section 6. Siting the Butts

i. The object of driving any game, but particularly grouse, is:

  a. To present the game to the guns so that it provides the most difficult and sporting shooting possible.
  b. At the same time it is most important to try to maintain control of the game and contact with it.
  c. A further drive may then be made including the same birds as well as additional fresh birds.

ii. This can sometimes be most satisfactorily accomplished so that the guns merely turn round and the game is driven back over them, BUT:

  a. It is usually better to move to other butts.
  b. The drive one way may be successful, but seldom is in both directions.

iii. The basis of this principle is finding out where the grouse prefer to fly in the first place:

  a. There are inevitably certain favoured sites, whether for feeding, shelter, or other reasons, to which the grouse in a particular area will move.
  b. The aim should then be to place the butts so that the grouse are driven over them to such a site. There should be more butts than guns to allow for alterations of winds.
  c. It may be possible then to drive the same birds back over the same butts, or else over a fresh line of butts sited on the same principle, with additional birds accompanying them.
  d. In this way contact is not lost with the game, and this is particularly important with grouse, because if the birds are allowed to scatter they may fly so far that the subsequent drives are spoiled.

Section 7. Points on Driving Grouse

i. The effects of the wind on some parts of the moor may be very much more noticeable than on another and this may always be utilised.

ii. Grouse prefer not to fly into the wind without good incentive, i.e. a particularly favoured feeding site.

iii. Grouse tend always to follow along the contours of hills rather than upwards and over obstacles, such as knolls.

iv. Though grouse may rise wild in a high wind they will usually be easier to drive if they are sheltering on lower ground from high winds on higher ground.

v. They will tend to be extremely reluctant to fly in very hot sunshine, or extremely hot drought conditions or heavy rain.

vi. After a sharp frost they may also tend to sit much tighter than before.

vii. Silence is the first essential of beaters at all times, but especially so when grouse are wild.

viii. Plans may be altered before the day begins, but once under way one badly managed drive when the birds fly wrongly is likely to affect the day far more than with other forms of shooting.

ix. Clever control of the angle or shape of the beating line and combined team work with flankers can funnel grouse where required, but it is easy to miscalculate.

Section 8. *Other points on the Moor*

i. An extremely useful asset on any grouse moor, when driving or at other times, is a pointing dog with a good nose.

    a. Knowledge of where the birds are, or have been, can be a tremendous asset when driving. It is then possible to head them in the right direction.

    b. Such a dog is useful to find nests and count birds accurately before the season opens.

    c. BUT it must be steady and well trained.

ii. It is quite easy to rear grouse, but when reared they remain tame and refuse to fly, except in packs.

iii. Experiments in feeding grouse have been tried, but have proved difficult, because of conditions. Grouse usually manage to feed where deer have pawed the ground clear.

iv. It is not possible for the moor keeper to know where more than a few of his birds nest because of the size of the area, and he must concentrate on protecting them from predators.

B. *Partridge Ground*

Section 1. *Knowledge of the Ground*

i. It is essential that the keeper, or organiser, on partridge ground should know the area intimately.

ii. He must know what crops are being grown and the various day-to-day farming movements which may affect his stock of birds:

    a. Hay cutting, or silage making, may mean nests being cut out and birds killed by the blades of the cutter.

    b. He should make arrangements with the tractor driver, possibly leaving a broody in a coop for him to slip eggs underneath if they are cut out.

    c. Cattle or sheep changing fields may mean altering plans for a shooting day.

    d. When hedges are being cut or trimmed it is often desirable to leave protective patches standing in places, or to trim them upwards, rather than keep them cut low.

    e. When the landowner also farms and shoots the area himself the situation is obviously ideal.

iii. He should know where his partridges' dusting places are, and where they are inadequate or unsafe, e.g. too close to a road, he should provide others.

iv. He should know the most suitable corners, or hedges, for feed hoppers, or for placing feed by hand, where it will do the maximum good for his birds and not be wasted on crows or other hungry mouths.

v. He should know the places where predators are likely to be encountered and act accordingly.

vi. A round of his ground should be a part of his daily routine.

Section 2. *Knowledge of the Birds*

It is most important that the keeper, or organiser, on partridge ground should know where all his birds are, or are likely to be, at all times of the year and at different times of the day.

i. During the shooting season he will know roughly the number of birds in each covey and also the number of coveys on his ground.

    a. After each shooting day he will observe the birds at feeding times and roughly estimate their numbers.

    b. He will be able also to make a rough estimate of numbers from the head in the bag, deducting mentally.

    c. He will never permit his stocks to become too low for future breeding, and he will make a point of sexing at least roughly the birds shot.

    d. At the same time his aim will be to take a sound proportion of the game crop and not leave too many birds on the ground.

ii. During the breeding season he will try to keep track of his birds as far as possible:

    a. As the birds pair in December–January it is an easy enough matter to observe roughly where each has its territory.

    b. It is possible for the experienced hand to guess the likely nesting sites in advance when this stage has been reached, or their approximate positions.

    c. It may be politic to provide suitable cover, if possible, where this may be lacking, e.g. a corner of a field fenced off, or some similar cover available. April–May is a busy time in this respect.

iii. When the birds are nesting it is inadvisable to disturb them more than is necessary:

    a. Nests in obviously exposed conditions may be provided with a little extra cover carefully applied as an added protection.

    b. Nests in obviously dangerous places where they will be cut-out, or disturbed in other ways before hatching, should be lifted and the eggs set under broodies.

    c. Regular over-close investigation of nesting sites may result in eggs being trampled on, or a path being made which will lead the hunting predator, or dog, straight to the nest.

    d. Protection against predators by regular patrolling and trapping is about the best that can be done. The rest must be up to the birds themselves.

iv. Inevitably there will be a considerable proportion of nests about which nothing can be done:

    a. Nests in the centre of corn fields which may be sprayed in June.

b. Nests which are in the centre of a field cut for hay or silage may be damaged or destroyed by accident.

c. Nests which have been overlooked by roadside or public pathway may also be damaged or destroyed, or the birds killed.

d. Predators will get their proportion of eggs in spite of all that the keeper or game preserver may do.

In spite of all this somehow a considerable proportion of the birds will succeed in hatching their young.

v. There must be a period from June onwards when the partridge keeper or game preserver simply keeps his fingers crossed.

a. Heavy rain and cold conditions on successive days after the chicks have hatched can kill off considerable numbers.

b. Prolonged drought at the same time may also result in many young chicks being lost.

c. Even when the chicks can fly after the first few weeks there are still constant hazards from predators and other sources.

d. Parent birds are most courageous in defence of their young and anyone who has seen the old birds beating a bewildered young dog or cat with their wings and setting it to flight, or defending their young against the repeated attacks of a hawk, or pair of crows, will have the utmost admiration for them, but this is not always enough.

vi. It is not until the crops are being cut and the coveys can be seen in the open that the game preserver can begin to assess accurately how many birds have been bred successfully.

Section 3. *Points on Driving*

There are many similar ties between driving grouse and partridges, but partridges have the advantage that if some drives go wrong it is usually not so important as it may be with grouse. There is usually more scope for alterations and last minute improvisations.

i. The basic principles involved are also very similar:

a. It is desirable to work on the principle of driving in a square, a rectangle or a circular fashion to aim at returning ultimately towards the starting point.

b. It is desirable to aim at driving the birds towards a likely holding cover, such as a field of roots.

  c. Several drives may be made with this object. The guns being placed between the fields being beaten and the holding cover.

  d. The aim should be to break the coveys up rather than drive them *en masse* over the guns.

  e. The ideal is to be able to place the guns in a square surrounded by holding cover on all four sides and to beat over them from each side in turn with two lots of beaters.

ii. The East Anglian partridge stand is usually:

  a. Marked by numbered sticks some 30 yards behind specially pruned hedges.

  b. These partridge driving hedges may be 10–15 feet high, providing good shots in front.

  c. The covey coming over them tightly will explode in all directions at the sight of the waiting guns.

iii. The downland driving of partridges may be very different and often more akin to grouse driving:

  a. Stands may be behind hurdles of wattle or camouflaged netting on posts, but these should be adequate. There is nothing worse than crouching behind inadequate cover.

  b. Such stands, as well as numbered sticks, may easily be blown down, knocked down by cattle, or otherwise affected, and the organiser should check accordingly.

  c. The guns may be stationed behind a stone dyke in some places, or close up to a hedge or fence in others. Again it is desirable that there should be sufficient cover for the gun to stand easily.

iv. Wherever a stand is in a ploughed field the organiser should stamp a flat area round it for the benefit of the gun. This should not be left for him to do, though it should be one of his first considerations if it has not been done.

v. Where guns are placed in hollows or gulleys it is particularly desirable that warning should be given of the advancing beaters. They might even carry flags as in grouse driving.

vi. The position of flankers should always be made clear to the outside guns.

vii. The wind is probably not as important in partridge driving as in grouse driving, but:

    a. It is easier to drive down wind than against the wind or across the wind.

    b. In extremely high winds driving may be almost impossible and plans may have to be adapted accordingly.

viii. Contours of the ground are not generally as important as in grouse driving, but again the tendency of the birds is to follow the contours of the ground.

    a. In flat country such as East Anglia this may not be of much importance, though a point to note.

    b. In downland country it is particularly noteworthy.

ix. When partridges can be driven over a strip of trees or similar obstacle they will present very pretty shooting.

    a. Even on the boundary it is well worth executing such a drive if possible.

    b. Although the aim should always be to keep the birds within bounds, they will return in the evening anyway.

    c. Driving over water, i.e. a stream or river, has the same effect of raising the birds.

Section 4. Rearing

Points of particular note are:

i.   It is questionable whether large scale rearing is always desirable. Dependent on the ground and circumstances, intensive conservation of wild stock is often preferable.

ii. Eggs may be successfully hatched in incubators. The chicks should be kept well supplied with water, grit and feed and allowed free range inside netted pens as soon as possible.

iii. It is most important not to give them range on ground that has been occupied by waterfowl, poultry or pheasants previously. There is a risk they may contract disease and die.

iv. Draught and weather-proof hutches are important, especially in the early stages before they are given free range.

v. As when approaching wild partridges with young, which are betraying the fact by typical wing trailing tactics, have a care not to tread on the youngsters in the pens. They are very small and active and can be easily overlooked.

vi. Control of predators near the pens is all important. One stoat, weasel or mink can cause havoc and some well placed tunnel traps alongside the pens are a desirable precaution.

vii. If small groups are put out round the shoot in pens and released gradually in twos and threes they should stay near the pen and acclimatise to the ground like wild birds. Artificial coveys may thus be settled around the shoot.

C. *Pheasant Coverts*

Section 1. Knowledge of the Ground

i. As with the partridge ground, it is essential that the game preserver knows his pheasant ground intimately.

ii. All the points covered in B, Section 1, above, concern him also in much the same degree.

iii. Apart from these points he must also consider matters relating solely to his coverts:

  a. No covert completely exposed to the winds and without any vestige of undergrowth will hold birds however much they may be fed in the way of grain.

  b. Sometimes certain otherwise attractive coverts in certain winds become cold and exposed and unattractive to the birds.

  c. If coverts are not adequately fenced cattle or sheep will disturb breeding birds, as well as grazing on protective vegetation.

  d. If suitable alternatives are not available he must try to plant protective hedges and suitable sheltering shrubs, such as snowberry, rhododendrons, etc., or shelter belts of kale, if possible.

  e. Undue thinning, or removal of undergrowth, should be resisted where possible compatible with the demands of efficient forestry. The two are usually quite compatible.

Section 2. Knowledge of the Birds

i. During the shooting season he will have a rough idea of the number of birds in his coverts.

  a. At feeding times the birds will appear and can be roughly counted and some sort of estimate made.

   b. A similar estimate may be made on the shooting days when the number of birds presented over the guns may be roughly estimated and the numbers in the bag at the end of the day may be mentally deducted.

   c. He will know at once when there has been a 'leak' of birds, due to:

      (*a*) An ineffective Stop on a shooting day.

      (*b*) Attractive feeding over the boundary.

      (*c*) The activities of poachers or predators.

      He will take steps to remedy matters.

ii. Shortly after the end of the shooting season he will be preparing his traps for breeding birds.

   a. These will be penned roughly in proportion of one cock to eight hens.

   b. Any surplus to requirements will be returned to the coverts.

   c. In due course he may take 35–45 eggs from each hen and when their duty is accomplished these birds may also be returned to coverts perhaps to rear a small wild brood.

iii. Ringing of reared birds can be helpful in learning the distances travelled by strays, but it seldom accounts for more than a small percentage of the birds shot by the end of the season.

iv. As with partridges, he will inevitably be unable to find more than a percentage of those birds laying wild, though he may have a shrewd idea of where many nests are.

   a. For the same reasons that it is inadvisable to search for partridge nests it is not always advisable to look too hard for pheasants' nests in safe areas.

   b. A good pointing dog can be a tremendous asset in finding both pheasant and partridge nests, even when the bird is sitting.

   c. A dog with a good nose will scent a sitting bird, even though supposedly without scent. Admittedly the scent may be reduced, but the birds can frequently be found in this way.

   d. This is a decided asset as once the location of a nest is thus indicated it can be pinpointed easily without disturbance and a distant watch kept on it.

   e. If it is desired to part branches or grass to find it a bendy hazel twig is best used.

    f. If the bird is nesting in a dangerous place the eggs must be lifted and placed under a broody. The hen pheasant will probably lay again elsewhere if caught early enough.

v. Rearing time is inevitably a busy period and the keeper or full-time game preserver rearing in any quantity will have little time to spare for anything else.

    a. He will not welcome visitors and should be left alone.

    b. The rearing field should never be visited with dogs; more especially dogs not under full control.

vi. Rearing has now been brought to such a pitch with the aid of mechanical brooders and special feeds that it is not much more difficult than rearing chickens, but:

    a. It is still a specialised business on a large scale.

    b. In spite of excellent remedies disease can take its toll if not checked promptly, or if the ground is not fresh.

    c. On a large scale it requires concentrated attention for two months at least.

    d. On a small scale any shoot could and should rear some birds.

vii. The introduction of the reared youngsters to the coverts is an anxious period until they have settled down to the new routine. Thereafter:

    a. The game preserver must continue to keep an eye open for predators.

    b. He must hope that the weather will not produce any freak storms which can cause havoc with young birds.

viii. As with partridges, the months of June–August are full of anxiety for the game preserver with a stock of pheasants. Nor can he tell how results are likely to be until the harvest is almost in.

Section 3. *Points on Driving*

Driving pheasants naturally has some similarities to driving both grouse and partridges, but basically there are three major differences:

i. Pheasants when they suspect danger are much more likely to squat or run, rather than fly. This tendency can be made use of in two obvious ways:

a. To shepherd the birds through the coverts in the required direction, pushing them along gently to the point where it is required they should fly, i.e. the flushing point.

b. To prevent them heading away from the coverts in directions unsuitable to the day's shooting, by providing well-sited stops. Hence also the effectiveness of sewelling.

ii. When once in flight pheasants are less likely than either grouse or partridges to swerve or turn back at the sight of the guns in front of them.

a. They will tend to head strongly for where they regard as home, i.e. their home coverts.

b. Or else they will head for other suitable coverts close at hand.

c. Likely alternative lines of flight may be assessed beforehand.

iii. The third major difference is that pheasants, given certain incentives, tend to climb upwards at the start of their flight.

a. This can be prompted either by flushing them from trees, or in front of water, thus causing the birds to rise and present high and difficult shots.

b. If an opposing covert to which the birds are flying is at an equal height to the one from which they are flushed, and the guns can be sited in a hollow between the two, this is obviously ideal.

iv. Flushing points should be placed in any coverts where it is desired to push birds out over the guns.

a. They should generally be sited at a suitable break in the trees, possibly amid bushes such as snowberry, rhododendrons or similar growth.

b. If a V of wire netting is set up with the open end towards the direction of the drive, birds can be easily flushed from this obstruction and forced to fly upwards through the clearing in the trees.

c. If it is desired to drive either way, a cross of wire netting will provide a flushing point from either angle.

d. Sewelling can provide a temporary flushing point, but care must be taken that a number of pheasants do not group together and too many take wing together.

    e. When too many birds are flushed in this way in a cloud over the guns it is impossible to shoot more than a few and indicates bad management. It is known as a bouquet.

    f. The object should be to flush the birds in small groups of two or three at a time in a steady flow over the guns. This can provide exciting shooting.

v. One major point that should always be borne in mind when planning any day is that birds will be very reluctant to fly directly into a strong wind.

    a. If a drive is planned without regard to this point the birds may all curl back over the beaters.

    b. It may however be that this can be utilised when planning a drive, relying on the birds not breaking into the wind.

    c. As with any form of driving, or shooting, the weather must always be a deciding factor in planning and execution.

Section 4. *Other points to note*

i. Sexing pheasants at the end of the day, or indeed during the shoot, presents little difficulty.

    a. Except sometimes in the case of a hen pricked in the ovaries which may show sex changes, growing the plumage and spurs of a cock. It will not breed.

    b. Hens should not be shot after December and the back-end cocks-only days should be conducted vigorously.

    c. It is rarely possible to shoot enough cocks towards the end of the season. Often a good plan to have a few cock-only days early in the season before they become wary.

ii. Ageing a pheasant is best done by the mandible test in the hens. Skull crushing will also indicate a young bird. The comparative age of cocks may be told by the size of their spurs. Small knobs indicate a bird of the year, long sharp daggers an old warrior.

PART 5

PREDATORS, TRAPS AND TRAPPING

Section 1. Protected Predators

The list of predators must inevitably be a lengthy one, but fortunately there are likely to be only a few species found on any particular shoot. Against some a ceaseless war should be waged. Against others no action may be taken because they are protected, as follows:

i. Golden Eagle:

   a. Will kill blue and brown hares and rabbits, also grouse. Is also a carrion eater.
   b. Traces of the kills, in the shape of the corpses, may be found in the nest.
   c. Its presence on a grouse moor can cause havoc during a drive.
   d. It kills on the ground, therefore grouse take to wing at sight.
   e. Restricted to Scottish moors in the Highlands; seldom seen farther south, though known in Cumberland.
   f. Apparently slowly increasing in numbers and range.

ii. Peregrine Falcon:

   a. Will kill any game bird on the wing. A most sporting spectacle.
   b. Kills may be identified when found by ring of feathers round the riven or headless corpse. Unmistakable.
   c. At one time endangered their numbers are now fully recovered. Chiefly found in wild rocky or coastal regions.

iii. Other Hawks and Harriers and Buzzards:

   a. Almost any of the above are likely to kill game chicks on the moor or elsewhere.
   b. There are not likely to be any traces left.
   c. Their presence near any release pens is therefore highly undesirable.

o   209

iv. Owls:

    a. Mainly nocturnal and beneficial.

    b. The Little Owl is an aggressive exception. The remarks applicable to iii. above also apply to this bird.

Section 2. Winged Predators not protected

i. The Hooded, or Carrion Crow:

    a. These are among the most widespread and deadly of predators, not only of game bird eggs and chicks, but of most other birds' eggs and chicks as well.

    b. They will quarter the ground or work along a hedge quite methodically during the breeding season and systematically clear the nests of eggs.

    c. They will also kill and eat young chicks and there will be no traces left.

    d. They must be shot, or trapped, whenever possible. May be shot over decoys, or mobbing a decoy owl.

    e. The Carrion Crow should not be mistaken for the Raven, which is protected. Ravens are larger, glossier versions of the same bird, but fortunately rare.

ii. The Greater Black-backed Gull:

    a. Has as voracious an appetite for eggs and chicks as the carrion crow and as much cunning.

    b. Can scarcely any longer be regarded as a sea bird in places and will nest far inland.

    c. Should be dealt with as firmly as the carrion crow.

iii. Rooks, Lesser Black-backed Gulls and Herring Gulls:

    a. In places where there are large numbers of rooks and gulls they may prove as bad as their relatives above.

    b. Their numbers should not be allowed to become excessive and their behaviour should be watched carefully.

iv. Magpies, Jackdaws and Jays:

    a. All three are cunning and persistent egg thieves.

    b. Each may be regarded as an enemy of the game preserver.

    c. Jays do have this advantage that they will give warning of the presence of any stranger, or predator, near a covert by their cries and behaviour. For this reason some game preservers like to have some in a wood.

Section 3. *Other Predators*

i. The Fox:

   a. Leaves obvious signs of his presence in the shape of the wings of his kill, neatly shorn off, and possibly some bloody remnants of his meal. Sometimes a half-buried half-eaten corpse.

   b. As well as game birds taken from their nests during the breeding season, or young chicks, the fox will eat rabbits, hares, mice, frogs and many other items.

   c. In a hunting county the question of killing foxes can usually be safely left to the hunt. It is important that those who hunt and those who shoot should each understand and respect each other's sports.

   d. In a non-hunting county foxes must be shot, trapped or gassed, although such methods may not be as effective or humane as instant death at the jaws of a pack of foxhounds.

ii. Wildcats:

   a. Only likely to be encountered on the fringes of moors in the highlands and now a fully protected species.

   b. Rabbits and hares are probably their principal food, although game birds no doubt may also be taken when available.

iii. Feral cats:

   a. High on the list of game predators must stand the hunting cat gone feral.

   b. A cat will cover a wider territory hunting than might be believed possible. 3–5 miles is not uncommon.

   c. They will kill and eat rabbits and leverets as well as game chicks, and birds as large as grouse and partridges.

   d. Traces will usually be left in the shape of identifiable scraps of bloodied fur, or feathers, but little else.

iv. Rats:

   a. Rats are voracious egg eaters and the enemies of game chicks

b. They should be exterminated by all available means, but modern methods of poisoning are most effective.

c. Traces of rats are usually visible at feeding places in the shape of scattered grain, droppings and paw marks. Runs and holes are usually obvious enough.

d. Warfarin left under cover at feeding points, whether rats are suspected or not, is a worthwhile precaution.

v. Stoats and Weasels:

a. The stoat is larger, with a black tip to the tail, otherwise they are often confused. There are however two sizes of weasel, one distinctly smaller.

b. Some game preservers argue that the only good stoat is a dead stoat.

c. Some also consider that weasels around farm buildings are a good insurance against rats.

d. Both are bloodthirsty killers and egg eaters. They will hunt rabbits and game chicks by scent. Their kills are usually notable for a bloody bite at the base of the neck. Sometimes quite a neat puncture. Where they have been eaten into this usually indicates the work of a stoat; where the blood has merely been sucked it is usually a weasel.

e. They are easily trapped, or may be enticed from their holes by imitating the squeal of an injured rabbit and then shot.

vi. Badgers:

a. Except in the case of occasional rogues, badgers seldom do significant harm to game. They very occasionally take a sitting bird or eat the eggs.

b. Signs of a badger's work are a disarranged nest with remains of smashed yolky or bloody eggshells visible amongst the ruins.

c. Apart from occasional lapses of this nature the badger is a harmless and interesting addition to any ground, protected by the Badger and the Wildlife and Countryside Acts.

vii. Hedgehogs:

a. Hedgehogs will on occasions disturb sitting birds and eat their eggs, but note:

b. Partially protected under the Wildlife and Countryside Act. It is thus illegal to set traps deliberately for them.

   c. But hedgehogs tend to blunder into traps which can be a nuisance: hence all entrances to traps should be sticked: i.e. protected with two sticks to keep them out.

viii. Moles:

   a. Though moles are not predators weasels have a habit of using mole runs.

   b. A sitting bird causes a warm patch, which attracts worms in the soil. This in turn attracts moles. They may then overturn the nest.

   c. Near known nests or rearing fields they are best trapped.

ix. Mink:

   a. This is a comparatively recent newcomer. The result of breeding amongst escapees from mink farms.

   b. It is both bloodthirsty and extremely savage for its size and now unfortunately quite common in parts of the country.

   c. Fortunately it is comparatively easy to trap.

x. Polecat:

   a. The true polecat is very rare, but, like the marten, not extinct by any means. They may not be deliberately trapped.

   b. Distinguishable by its size and staggeringly powerful smell.

Section 4. Cage Traps

i. Cage traps for birds work on the lobster-pot principle, i.e. they have one, or sometimes two, entrances through which a bird may get in, but is unable to get out.

   a. It is illegal to bait them with live birds, but they may be baited with suitable feeding and the first attracts others.

   b. Corvines, crows, rooks, jays and jackdaws are the principal quarry.

ii. Cage traps of this kind must be large enough to hold a good number of birds and to provide access to remove them, i.e. a doorway for the trapper to enter.

iii. They are made of wire netting on a wooden frame and may be of varying size and degrees of permanency.

   a. They can be transportable.

   b. They may be set up on a semi-permanent basis.

iv. A form of cage trap is usually used by the game preserver to collect game birds for breeding purposes at the end of the season.

v. Small portable cage traps, of varying sizes with fall doors, are sometimes used for trapping.

  a. They have advantages where it is desired not to mark the pelt, e.g. in the case of mink.

  b. They also have the advantage that the quarry is caught alive and unharmed, which may be desirable; e.g. in the case of domestic cats out hunting, which can then be returned to the owner with a warning.

  c. They have the disadvantage that they are bulky and heavy to carry about.

  d. They have the disadvantage that they are not always easy to conceal and they tend to hold the smell of humans.

vi. This type of cage trap may be home constructed, but they must be toughly built if for instance intended to hold a mink or a fox.

vii. Permanent cage traps of this kind are sometimes to be found in stone dyke countries for foxes. A combination of this and deadfall traps, i.e. the stone to close them is poised to fall.

Section 5. Deadfall Traps

i. Now of dubious legality, but may still be used in stone wall country where suitable flat slabs are easily found to make them.

ii. They consist basically of a flat stone slab so poised that at the slightest touch it falls on top of the victim.

iii. The simplest of all is the heavy stone slab propped on edge with a baited twig to support it.

  a. To reach the bait the victim has to reach up and must move the twig.

  b. Then the slab falls and instantly crushes the victim.

  c. This is sometimes known as the Dr. Deadfall and in spite of being primitive it is surprisingly effective.

iv. Another well-known deadfall trap is that known as the Figure Four trap, due to the fact that when set the three wooden supports used in it form a figure four. They consist of:

  a. A sharpened base support, which is stuck upright in the ground.

b. A cross piece notched in the centre to fit a corresponding notch in the centre of the upright base support.

c. A lateral spar, the lower end of which fits into a notch in the end of the cross-piece, while its centre rests on top of the base piece.

d. The whole is kept in position by the weight of the stone slab leaning against this lateral spar.

e. When a bait on the cross piece is touched the whole edifice collapses abruptly on the victim.

Section 6. *Tunnel Traps*

i. It is desirable to make any trap as selective as possible, i.e. only to trap those animals for which the trap is intended.

ii. For this reason no trap must be set in the open uncovered where it might catch any animal stumbling upon it. N.B.: This has been the cause of many game bird deaths in the past.

iii. It is the natural inclination of any small animals such as rats, weasels and stoats to follow certain obvious convenient tracks or runs.

iv. Where such tracks can be joined by a convenient tunnel it can be certain they will use it with alacrity.

v. Such tunnels are therefore deadly sites for traps and traps thus placed are known as tunnel traps.

vi. Such tunnels may be constructed from almost any materials convenient to hand, e.g. a slate leaned against a stone dyke.

vii. Where a tunnel trap is elaborately constructed it is important that the materials used should not smell of man's scent, or else be given time to weather.

viii. The top of the tunnel should be readily removable to provide access to the trap beneath.

ix. The ordinary approved Fenn vermin trap is built on much the same principle as the now illegal gin trap, i.e. the animal steps on a platform which actuates the mechanism.

x. Such traps should themselves be covered with soil once set, though bare traps may be quite adequate.

Section 7. *Noose Traps, or Snares*

i. These are generally constructed of light picture wire with a brass eyehole as a runner.

ii. When used for snaring rabbits they also require:

    a. A stout cord attaching this firmly to a peg.

    b. The support of a cleft stick about 6 inches long known as a tealer, in which the wire is set at the right angle so that the loop of the snare correctly covers the rabbit's run.

iii. When snaring rabbits the snare is traditionally set 'a hand's breadth high' and for snaring hares half a hand higher. This is as good a rough measure as any.

iv. Such snares are best set 'pear shaped' rather than round as they will run more readily and there is less chance of them sticking.

v. It is best to knot the snares so that they do not close beyond a certain point.

    a. If the snare has been cunningly set it may well be that the animal's neck has been broken.

    b. If it is not killed thus when caught in a knotted snare it will not struggle, but will lie quietly until the arrival of the snarer.

    c. If the snare is not knotted it will be strangled into unconsciousness and then will relax, when the hold of snare will release it sufficiently to allow it to recover and be slowly strangled again.

    d. Rabbits killed thus have an unpleasant bulging-eyed appearance.

vi. Snares are sometimes set on fencing wire direct to save trouble.

    a. But many other animals, including pheasants and other game birds, may use rabbit runs to slip under a fence.

    b. They are liable to thrust their heads through such a rabbit snare and be choked to death.

    c. They are a lazy man's way of snaring and should not be allowed on any shoot.

vii. Another method of setting such a snare, generally for rats in their runs, is to attach it to a stout hazel switch.

    a. This is stuck firmly in the ground and then bent over until the snare can be set at the required angle in the run.

    b. A peg with a hook top is inserted in the ground and a similar peg attached to the cord of the snare is then hooked on to it.

c. The hazel wand is then held bent over under the strain and the noose is set at the right angle over the run.

d. When the animal runs into the noose it pulls the peg free and the hazel wand promptly straightens up and the animal is left hanging.

e. This is known descriptively as 'a bender'.

Section 8. *Points on Trapping and Snaring*

i. Snares for foxes can be a very effective means of control, but self-locking snares are illegal.

ii. All traps and snares must be inspected once a day by law and any animal caught removed.

iii. Before setting any traps the trapper should always rub his hands well with soil to dull the human scent. He should do the same with the traps themselves.

iv. It is inhumane as well as illegal to set any spring trap in the open. It may catch or injure a domestic animal or bird.

v. The approved successors to the old illegal gin trap are:

a. The Fenn: Mks. III, IV and VI. Two jaws work on coil springs. Small, compact and easily set in confined spaces.

b. Mks. III and IV are suitable for stoats, weasels, rats and squirrels. Mk. VI will kill mink and adult rabbits. Also:

c. The Imbra: no longer made: for small ground predators, mink and rabbits: larger, with two scissor action jaws: needed more room to set. Awkward to set in a tunnel. Also:

d. The Juby trap, now also out of production. Similar scissor action, but stronger and operated by two coil springs.

e. When used for rabbits both these must be set well within the overhang of a burrow.

f. It is important with any of these traps to remember to unset the safety catch before leaving them in position.

g. No longer made and less well known are the Sawyer trap, looks similar to the Fenn, and the Lloyd trap, working on similar principles to the old gin, but with overlapping jaws. Both restricted to catching small ground predators.

h. There is still scope for the inventor in this field.

vi. The trapper should always keep an eye open for signs of predators on his ground and be ready to set a trap in a likely place.

vii. There should be certain 'main road' runs and junctions where tunnel traps can be set on a more or less permanent basis and can be assured of constantly catching their quota.

viii. Regular records of trapping results should be kept.

ix. The basis of baiting on all traps should either be:

    a. Sex. A female stoat or weasel trailed along a ditch will be certain to lead several males into a trap or traps sited there. Or if hung on a convenient twig with a trap underneath this is likely to be successful.

    b. Hunger. A tasty morsel such as the paunch of a freshly killed rabbit trailed over likely ground in the same manner and then used as bait is likely to ensure good results.

x. A gallows, i.e. a rotting row of shrivelling carcases of small predators such as stoats and weasels, which is often to be seen on view near keepers' houses, serves no useful purpose beyond possibly impressing a credulous employer.

    a. An accurate tally can and should be kept without the need for this grisly display.

    b. The animals themselves would probably serve a better function used as bait for further traps.

    c. They breed flies and stink. They are better buried.

PART 6

THE DOG AND HIS TRAINING

Section 1. The Choice of a Dog

The gun dog should be as indispensable an adjunct to shooting as a gun. To find the game to shoot, to find it when it has been shot, and to remedy any bad shooting by retrieving wounded game, a gun dog is essential. But as the gun should match the man so the gun dog should as far as possible match the shooting. The Kennel Club divides gun dogs into the following categories:

i. Retrievers. This includes:

   a. Black and yellow Labradors.
   b. Golden Retrievers.
   c. Flat, or Curly Coated Retrievers.
   d. Chesapeakes.

ii. Pointers and Setters. This includes:

   a. English Pointers.
   b. English, Irish and Gordon Setters.

iii. Spaniels. This includes:

   a. English or Welsh Springers.
   b. Clumbers.
   c. Cockers.
   d. Sussex.
   e. Irish Water Spaniels.

iv. German Shorthaired Pointers and those breeds which hunt, point and retrieve. This includes:

   a. Weimaraners.   *c.* Munsterlanders.
   b. Magyar Vyszlas,   *d.* Wirehaired Pointers.
       i.e. Hungarian Pointers.

Section 2. The Preliminaries

It has been said that each man gets the gun dog he deserves, but at least it should be possible to start well.

i. Having decided on the type of gun dog most suited to the type of shooting he is doing—and this must be a personal matter for everyone to decide for himself—he should:

    a. Find out something about the breed selected, if he does not already know very much.

    b. The breed secretary will usually be very willing to help and advise on dogs or pups available.

ii. Having confirmed his initial decision he should then:

    a. Decide whether he has time or ability to train his dog himself; or

    b. Decide whether or not to buy a trained dog.

    c. Look around and see a few of the dogs and pups which are available.

iii. When looking at any possible purchase he should try to find out:

    a. How the sire and dam work, and if possible see them working.

    b. What other progeny of the same breeding have turned out like, if it is a pup he is contemplating buying.

iv. To ensure reasonable results he should buy:

    a. A pure-bred rather than a cross-bred dog, registered at the Kennel Club, as this implies a certain standard if nothing more.

    b. From reputable breeders who have a reputation to maintain.

    c. Cross-bred dogs may or may not live up to their reputation for intelligence and may or may not be good workers, but they will seldom breed good progeny.

Section 3. The Early Days

Having bought either a pup or a trained dog, he should:

i. See that he has it comfortably kennelled in a warm dry kennel with a good run;

ii. Or if he is keeping it in the house, ensure that it has a private corner and basket of its own.

iii. He must start at once, whether pup or trained dog, to get to know the animal.

iv. If he has bought a trained dog from a reputable trainer the latter will probably have tried:

   a. To show him the exact words, whistles and signals used as commands.

   b. To show him the dog working and get them to work together.

   c. To emphasise, if he has not already realised the fact, that although the dog is trained it cannot be expected to work at once with a new owner.

v. To settle in a young pup in strange surroundings:

   a. It should be rubbed all over with the straw or blanket used for a bed so that it does not have a strange smell to it.

   b. Warm milk and an aspirin crushed in it will usually help, but howls should be resolutely ignored.

Section 4. *The Initial Training*

Assuming that a young pup has been bought and that it is to be trained, it should be appreciated—

i. No great amount of expensive equipment is required, merely—

   a. A collar and lead.

   b. A length of stout cord.

   c. Some easily manufactured dummies for retrieving made from either: old socks stuffed with soft material, or a roll of canvas similarly stuffed.

   d. A blank pistol, or a blank adaptor for the gun, either of which may be cheaply obtained from a gunsmith.

   e. A suitable paddock or open space free of distractions.

ii. Nor is a great amount of time required:

   a. A short period morning and evening should suffice.

   b. Regularity without monotony is important. The pup should appreciate a routine and look forward to its training.

iii. Some advocate not starting training until the pup is at least nine months old, but a great deal depends on the puppy and the breed. It should be studied carefully.

   a. If it is a nervous and shy pup care must be taken to guide it gently on the right lines.

   b. If it is a bold and boisterous pup it may be possible to take it along faster.

   c. In either case the owner should get to know it really well before trying too much. Too many pups have been spoiled by pushing too hard too young.

iv. On the other hand, the initial training should start from the earliest days:

a. At meals the bowl should be held above the pup and it should be encouraged to sit, with the command 'Sit'.

b. It should also gradually be encouraged to sit to the raised hand and long whistle, or similar sound; ultimately blanks.

v. When led out for walks on the lead:

a. It should be encouraged to maintain the 'at heel' position with the command 'heel'.

b. But the lead should never be allowed to signify loss of liberty in the pup's mind. It should be slipped on and off at intervals.

c. It should learn to know its name, which should be a clear, short, easily pronounced one, preferably monosyllabic.

d. It should be encouraged to run to the handler when called and made much of when it does; a hand tapping the knee and a short whistle repeated may be substituted for the name, plus the command 'Heel'.

e. In the very early stages concrete rewards in the way of biscuit or similar titbits may be provided, but later it should simply be patted.

vi. It must be appreciated that tone of voice and the human eye are most important factors, which can affect a puppy very considerably.

vii. In no circumstances must the temper ever be lost with a pup, however tiresome it may be. If there is any danger of this, take it home at once.

viii. It must be appreciated that all training may take time:

a. Also no training every goes on straightforwardly always.

b. There are bound to be days when everything seems wrong and the pup most disobedient. They are better ignored, but try to finish such days with a simple command correctly obeyed.

c. Never, on the one hand, give a command and let the pup get away without obeying it, if it is aware that it is being disobedient.

d. Never, on the other hand, nag. Especially do not give pointless orders and needless repetition.

e. Be content with a little at a time and slow but steady progress. It may take months, but so does any schooling.

ix. When this initial period is complete:

    a. The pup should sit to command, signal whistle and shot.

    b. The pup should come to heel and walk at heel to command, signal and whistle.

    c. If this groundwork has been correctly laid it is half-way to being a trained dog.

Section 5. *Initial Retrieving*

With the dog that has a high degree of natural instinct it will hardly be necessary to do more than encourage the instinct on the right lines:

i. If the pup picks up old bones or smelly, decaying birds or similar relics and brings them, do not scold it, or it may be put off retrieving. Accept it, saying 'Dead', and make much of the pup.

ii. The pup may be encouraged to carry from the earliest days if necessary by providing it with a toy.

iii. Once it will carry the first retrieving lesson may take place near the kennel, or basket.

    a. The handler should stand between kennel or basket and the pup and throw the dummy or chosen object a short way.

    b. At the same time he should encourage the pup to run in and pick it up.

    c. It will almost certainly then pick it up and run with it towards its kennel or basket.

    d. It should be gently intercepted, made much of, and the dummy, or chosen object, taken gently from it, saying at the same time 'Dead'.

    e. If the pup is reluctant to give it up, the lips may be very gently squeezed against the teeth, but care must be taken not to hurt the pup.

iv. In due course the lesson may be extended to throwing the dummy into long grass out of sight and restraining the pup from running in at once, until the command 'Hie Lost' or 'Fetch' is given.

v. When the pup has mastered this and is enjoying his lessons the dummy may be dropped clearly in the pup's view, he may then be led on for several paces before the command 'Hie Lost' is given.

    a. The distance walked away may be gradually increased eventually to over 100 yards.

    b. In due course in this manner the pup learns to follow his first scent trail as well as retrieve.

Section 6. More Advanced Training

i. The more advanced training for retrieving consists of:

    a. Using two dummies, then three or more, thrown in turn in full view of the dog, to teach him to mark the fall of game.

    b. Teaching him to respond to hand signals by finding dummies laid out beforehand for 'blind' retrieves. Also thus encouraging him to use his nose.

    c. He is taught to retrieve dead game, starting on a close feathered bird such as a duck with the wings bound by an elastic band to encourage him to take it up correctly at once.

    d. He is taught to follow a scent trail laid with the aid of fishing line and a helper to avoid the trail being foiled, or in case he tries to follow the handler's scent.

ii. He is encouraged to quarter his ground and to hunt in the manner he will be expected to work in the field; i.e. either close in, within range of the gun, or well out beyond range of the gun, if expected to point the game.

iii. If he is to point the instinct will probably be well developed and will merely require drawing out:

    a. A check cord may be used to ensure that the game is not flushed prematurely.

    b. The use of a tame pigeon with the head tucked under the wing, and the wing drawn down behind the legs 'locking' it in position until flushed, is helpful.

    c. Or the pigeon may be 'dizzied' by rocking with the head under the wing, while held between the hands. It should then be placed carefully on the ground.

d. The dog is then brought up within scenting range of the bird downwind on the check lead.

e. He should be held still as soon as he catches the scent and gently stroked all over by the handler. He should be held there for some time. In due course when the instinct manifests itself fully he should become a staunch pointer.

Section 7. *Work in the Field*

Initially the work with the gun dog in the field during the first season should largely consist of more advanced training:

i. The handler and gun dog should be working as two parts of a team and they should be constantly learning from and with each other.

ii. Each day out with the gun and with each other should mean something fresh learned.

iii. The ultimate aim should be complete sympathy and understanding between them, as well as mastery of each of their respective roles.

iv. This cannot be achieved without hard work on both their parts; in very few cases is it every fully achieved, but the attempt is worth making.

   a. The handler should forget about his gun and concentrate on his dog for a while.

   b. He should take his dog picking-up and in the process he will learn a great deal about shoot management and shooting, as well as the behaviour of game.

   c. He should work his dog while other guns shoot over him. Again, both he and the dog will learn a great deal.

v. It is not suggested that this is more than a brief outline of what is required, or of the torments and pleasures involved in dog training.

   a. For fuller accounts of dog training or shooting over dogs the reader is referred to the bibliography.

   b. It should however be sufficient to indicate that the game shot will find this yet another aspect of his sport in which he will find much satisfaction.

   c. There can be few greater pleasures in shooting than watching one's own dog, or dogs, retrieving successfully after finding and flushing the game in the first instance.

P

PART 7

POINTS OF NOTE

Section 1. The 1968 Firearms Act

The 1988 Firearms (Amendment) Act, amending the 1968 Act, is now in force and should be studied carefully. Under this Act it is necessary for anyone wishing to own a shotgun to apply for a shotgun certificate at his local police station:

i. The application must be attested by:
    a. An M.P., J.P., Minister, Doctor, Lawyer, Bank Official or person of similar standing.
    b. Other than a member of the applicant's family.

ii. It is a serious offence to make a false statement to obtain a certificate and is punishable with up to six months in prison and/or a fine of up to £200.

iii. The police will not grant a certificate:
    a. To anyone who has been sentenced to more than three years in prison or corrective training.
    b. To anyone within five years of a three months' prison sentence or Borstal training.
    c. If there is a danger to public safety or of a breach of the peace.

iv. The police in most areas pay visits to all shotgun certificate holders to ensure:
    a. That guns and cartridges are kept suitably secure.
    b. That the circumstances remain the same.

v. The certificate costs £12 initially for a three year period.
    a. Renewal, or replacement if lost, costs £8.
    b. A visitor to the U.K. wishing to use a shotgun should apply for a certificate through a resident in the area.

Section 2. Wildlife and Countryside Act 1981

All wild birds are protected except the following during the particular periods specified:

Capercaillie from 1st October to 31st January.

Common Snipe from 12th August to 31st January.

Game Birds:

Grouse and Ptarmigan from 12th August to 10th December.

Blackgame 20th August to 10th December.

Partridge from 1st September to 1st February.

Pheasant from 1st October to 1st February.

Also:

Inland from 1st September to 31st January, or on the Foreshore from 1st September to 20th February (i.e. 'in or over any area below the high water mark of ordinary Spring tides'):

Wildfowl:	Wild Geese:
Common Pochard	Canada
Gadwall	Greylag
Golden Eye	Pinkfoot
Mallard	Whitefront
Pintail	
Shoveller	
Teal	
Tufted Duck & Wigeon	

Also:

From 1st September to 31st January:

Coot

Golden Plover

Moorhen

Woodcock in Scotland, but from 1st October to 31st January in England and Wales.

The following are birds which may be shot at any time of the year by an authorised person, i.e.

i. Landlord, Tenant, or person having the shooting rights.

ii. Or person with permission from one of these.

iii. Or person authorised in writing, by the Local Authority, or Statutory bodies such as the Nature Conservancy, River Boards, Local Fishery Committees, etc.

Carrion Crow	Domestic pigeon gone feral
Greater Black-backed Gull	House Sparrow
Lesser Black-backed Gull	Magpie

Rook	Herring Gull
Jackdaw	Jay
Starling	Wood-pigeon & Collared dove

N.B. Shooting any wild bird in Scotland on Sunday or Christmas Day is illegal and such prohibitions may be in force in any county in England and Wales by order of the Secretary of State.

Also:

i. The Secretary of State is empowered to alter these schedules and either add any bird to them or remove it from them by order.

ii. Thus open seasons may be further restricted in any area or in severe weather conditions they may be restricted for a particular bird or birds.

iii. If there is any question as to whether such an order is in force enquiries should be made at the nearest police station.

v. The holder of a shotgun certificate must inform the police at once if any shotgun in his possession is stolen.

vi. A shotgun is defined as a smooth bore gun other than an air weapon, with a barrel of not less than 24 inches.

    a. It is an offence to give a shotgun to anyone under fifteen.

    b. No one under the age of seventeen is allowed to buy a shotgun or shotgun ammunition.

    c. A loaded shotgun may not be carried in a public place.

Section 3. The Law and the Game Licence

Before any person may kill grouse, blackgame, moorgame, partridges, pheasants, hares, rabbits, woodcock or snipe, he must first have a Game Licence.

i. All Game Licences expire on 31st July of each year, except 14-day licences obtainable at £2, current only for a 14-day period. But N.B.:

    a. No game licence is required for killing rabbits on enclosed ground with the permission of the owner or tenant farmer, but any trespasser killing rabbits without a game licence is committing an offence.

    b. No game licence is required for killing hares or rabbits by a farmer, or persons authorised by him.

    c. It is just as much an offence to use a gun with the intention of shooting game as it is to shoot game. It is therefore no excuse to have missed the game. Fine may be £20.

ii. If a person is doing anything for which a game licence is required his licence may be demanded by:

   a. A revenue, or police, officer.

   b. The owner, landlord, lessee, or occupier of the land.

   c. Any other person possessing a game licence,

   N.B.: The licence must be shown and name and address given on demand. If not produced penalty may be £20.

Section 4. Societies, Organisations and Publications

i. The British Field Sports Society. Its aims are:

   a. The furtherance of all field sports.

   b. Opposing anti-field sports propaganda by the misguided.

   c. Assisting members and especially the young by guidance and well-written booklets.

   All sportsmen should be members.

ii. The British Association for Conservation and Shooting: the largest organisation in Britain concerned solely with shooting.

   a. It has around 200 affiliated local clubs throughout the country.

   b. It is not merely concerned with wildfowling, but with inland roughshooting clubs as well.

   c. It is concerned with protecting the rights of its members.

   d. It organises the rearing and ringing of wildfowl.

iii. The Game Conservancy, Fordingbridge, Hants. Open to all: Provides vital habitat and shooting research: Members receive:

   a. Annual report and three news letters covering recent research on new game management methods, effects of pesticides, hedges for nesting, predators, hares, roe deer, grouse ecology, woodcock behaviour, wildfowl, etc.

   b. Any shoot surveyed for practical game management advice. Advice by telephone/letter and quick post mortem service.

   c. Courses, lectures, meetings, group activities, technical symposia and social events at county level for all ages.

v. Publications. Great Britain:

   Weekly: *The Shooting Times*. (Official organ of B.A.S.C.)
   Country Life.

> *Shooting News.*
> *Sporting Gun.*
Monthly: *The Field.*
> *The Shooting Life.*
> *Countrysport.*
Annual: *The Shooter's Year Book.*
Overseas. U.S.A.:
Weekly: *Field and Stream.*
> *Outdoor Life.*

Section 5. Glossary of Technical Terms used in Game Shooting

Acknowledge flush: when a hunting dog drops to flushed game.

Action: that part of the gun which connects the stock to the barrels and contains the mechanism for firing the cartridges.

Anvil: that part of the interior of the cap of the cartridge which receives the impact of the striker pin.

Back: when one pointer, or setter, honours the point of another on sight and comes on point also.

Bag: the head of game plus 'Various' shot during the day.

Barrels: the cylindrical steel tubes in which the cartridges are inserted and through which the shot travels.

Beaters: those who drive the birds over the guns.

Beater's gun: one who walks with the beaters to take the birds which break back.

Bender: a wire snare attached to a bent hazel wand, so that when an animal is caught in the snare the wand straightens.

Blackgame: Blackcock and greyhen.

Blink: can mean not remaining staunch on point, e.g. returning to handler, or can mean failing to point game.

Blow-back: half burned, or burning grains of powder after a shot.

Bouquet: a number of pheasants crossing the guns in a mass.

Box-lock: the simplest, most easily adjusted and best known of mechanisms for firing the cartridge.

Brace: a pair of any game.

Brace work: two working in unison; of gundogs.

Break cover: to leave the shelter of cover and enter the open; of ground game in front of beaters.

Break field: to enter a field before the handler; of a gun dog.

Brown: to fire into a covey of birds without selecting a bird.

Buck: male hare or rabbit.

Butt: a prepared position for a gun to stand awaiting driven grouse.

Cartridge case: is a closed cylinder with a flange at one end designed to fit inside the cartridge chamber of the gun and containing the charge and primer.

Cast-off: when the stock has a bend to the right of the line of the barrels to align the barrels with the vision.

Cast-on: when the stock has a bend to the left to align the barrels with the vision. Usually in left shoulder gun.

Cheeper: A young game bird.

Choke: A very slight constriction towards the end of the barrels which has the effect of concentrating the shot as it leaves the barrels.

Clapped: Squatting 'frozen' to avoid danger; of game.

Clean delivery: game delivered to hand without mouthing or excitement; of a gun dog.

Clean pick-up: game retrieved steadily without mouthing or hesitation; of a gun dog.

Cock: male bird, or short version of woodcock.

Coney: a rabbit.

Covert: a wood.

Covey: a group of partridges or grouse: not more than a 'family' size.

Cut-off: when the paper case of a cartridge has been separated from the brass head inside the gun.

Doe: female hare or rabbit.

Draw on: advance steadily on point towards game; of gun dogs.

Drumming: noise made by a snipe's tail feathers vibrating.

Euston system: now almost obsolete method of hatching partridges by removing the eggs and replacing with dummies until on the point of hatching.

False pointing: pointing where no game lies; of gun dogs.

Fitchet: polecat/ferret cross.

Flanker: beater with a flag whose job is to turn any covey of grouse or partridge attempting to break sideways.

Flighting: shooting wildfowl by waiting on feeding lines at dawn or dusk.

Flush: to cause game to take flight.

Flushing point: a place where birds are forced to take flight from a covert, due either to the presence of sewelling, or wire netting.

Form: scrape where a hare lies in the open.

Forward allowance: the theoretical amount allowed in front of a crossing bird.

Fouling: the deposit left in the barrels after a shot has been fired.

Game: blackgame, grouse, partridge, pheasant, ptarmigan.

Gin trap: form of leg trap, based on old man-trap, now illegal.

Grey partridge: common partridge.

Gun: used in field to refer to the man carrying the gun.

Gun-fitting: see Try-gun.

Heel scent: the scent track leading away from game.

Hide: a small artificially built place of concealment for the gun when shooting pigeons or wildfowl.

Hob: a male ferret.

Hocked: hind tendon of ground game nicked after legging to prevent the legs slipping apart.

Hoe: old command used to steady dog on point: corruption of Toho: in itself corruption of Soho used in hare coursing.

Hold game: keep game fixed by staunch pointing; of gun dogs.

Improved cylinder: a barrel with five points of choke.

Jack: male hare.

Jag: attachment screwing on to cleaning rod to hold tow to clean barrels.

Jill: female ferret.

Jug, Juk or Jouk: roosting on ground of partridges or pheasants.

Jugging, jouking or jukking circle: position of roosting indicated by droppings; of partridges.

Kindle: to bear young; of rabbits.

Leash: three of a species.

Legged: Hind leg slit and other thrust through for carrying; of ground game.

Lek: ground on which blackgame carry out mating.

Lekking: the mating performance of blackgame.

Lie-up: when ferret remains down the hole.

Line ferret: ferret attached to knotted line to locate lie-up.

Long drop: to drop at a distance from handler on command; of gun dog.

Magnum: a gun chambered for larger cartridges than normal in that bore or gauge.

Mark: noting where game falls.

Melanistic mutant: dark type of pheasant with pale soles to feet.

Muse or Meuse: gap in hedge or fence where hare goes through.

Nitro-proof: the process of proving a gun safe for use with nitro powders.

Nye: a brood of young pheasants.

Pair: to mate; of partridges and grouse.

Pattern: the density of shot at the target.

Peg: when a hunting dog seizes squatting game.

Percussion cap: cap in base of cartridge which contains the detonator compound.

Planing: gliding downwards with set wings; usually of pheasants.

Plating: firing a barrel at a whitewashed steel plate to check the pattern of shot thrown.

Pneumatic wad: expanding card wad used instead of felt or compound.

Point: to indicate the presence of game by rigid stance; of gun dogs.

Poke: to aim with the gun instead of swinging.

Pricked: wounded birds, which have been hit by pellets.

Proof-marks: The record of proving stamped on the barrels by the proof house testing the gun.

Purse net: net to fit over holes formed like old-fashioned draw-string purse; designed to close tight when rabbit bolts.

Quartering: an efficient method of hunting the ground combining maximum use of nose and game-finding qualities; of gun dogs.

Red-legged partridge: the French partridge.

Right and left: two birds killed by two barrels fired without gun leaving shoulder.

Road out: to work out scent to ensure game has all gone after being flushed; of gun dogs.

Rocketer: a fast climbing and accelerating pheasant, or other game bird, coming over the gun.

Roughshoot: a shoot where there is no full-time keeper and game is not reared on any scale nor regularly driven over the guns by organised beaters.

Run: track left by rabbit or hare, or sometimes other game.

Run-in: when a dog runs forward, without orders, after game.

Runner: a winged bird capable of running on the ground.

Safety catch: a slide, usually on top of the stock, which merely acts as a check on the triggers.

Seat: where a rabbit lies in the open.

Sewelling: cord knotted with cloth, etc.; to flush pheasants.

Sewin: alternative term for sewelling.

Snap caps: dummy cartridges to prevent strikers being damaged if triggers are pulled.

Spurs: claws of cock pheasant.

Stop: man stationed to prevent birds breaking out.

Striker: the pin which causes detonation of the percussion cap.

Stringing of shot: the column of shot on way to target.

Strong on wing: when young birds are able to fly well and boldly.

Swing: movement of gun across body at speed of crossing bird.

Tealer: wooden cleft-stick support for a snare.

Towered bird: a bird which flies almost perpendicularly after being shot in the lung or spine, before dropping stone dead.

Trace: the footprint of a hare in the snow.

True cylinder: a barrel which is completely unchoked.

Try-gun: a gunsmith's gun which can be adjusted for fitting.

Turks Head: a woollen mop attachment to the cleaning rod, used for oiling barrels.

Various: species of birds or animals not specifically mentioned in the columns of a game register.

Vermin: commonly used to describe animals destructive of game.

Wad: disc of felt or similar material which prevents gas escaping past the shot charge.

Walking up: guns walking in line to flush partridges, etc.

Wildfowling: flight shooting and punt gunning after wildfowl.

Winged bird: a bird shot in the wing and incapable of flying.

Section 6. A Brief Annotated Chronological Outline and Bibliography of Game Shooting

Game shooting with guns dates only from the time of the Tudors.

1509 Henry VIII came to the throne. Matchlocks the only guns.

1520 The wheel-lock was invented in Nuremburg.

1533 An Act was passed whereby 'None shall shoot with or keep in his house any cross-bow, handgun ... unless he hath lands to the value of £100 per annum'. Guns had to be 'under a yard in length'.

1547 Edward VI.

1548 'An Acte against the shooting of Hayle Shotte: There ys growen a customable manner of shotinge of hayleshotte, whereby an infynite sorte of fowle ys killed and much Game thereby destroyed to the benefytt of no man.'

1553 Mary.

1558 Elizabeth I.

1603 James I.

1604 An Act restricting shooting: 'That all and everie person and persons which from and after the 1st day of August following shall shoote, destroye, or kill with any Gunne, Crossbow, Stonebow, or Longbow any Phesant, Partridge, House Dove, or Pigeon. Hearne, Mallard, Duck, Teale, Wigeon, Grouse, Heathcocks, Moregame, or any such Fowle, or any Hare.'

1621 *Hunger's Prevention*, or the Whole Arte of Fowling by Water and Land, by Gervase Markham. Includes the first mention of dog training, retrieving and setting.

1625 Charles I.
An English version of the flintlock had been developed.

1642–46 The first Civil War.

1648 The second Civil War between Parliament and the Army. Matchlocks and wheel locks still in common use.

1649 Charles I executed.

1660 Charles II. More advanced ideas on shooting probably brought with him from the Continent.

1674 *The Gentleman's Recreation in Hawking, Hunting, Fowling, Fishing and Agriculture*, by Nicholas Cox. Recommended not 'shooting against the wind' and to use a gun 'of five and a half to six feet in length'.

1685 James II.

1686 *The Gentleman's Recreation*, treating of Horsemanship, Hawking, Hunting, Fowling, Fishing and Agriculture. The second edition with a third section on Forest, Chace and Game Laws also included the first mention of 'Shooting Flying': 'It is now the mode to shoot flying as being by Experience found the best and surest Way.'

1689 William and Mary.

1707 Act of Union.

1709 *Game Law and of Hawking, Hunting, Fishing and Fowling*, by Giles Jacob.

1713 Treaty of Utrecht ended War of Spanish Succession. The returning officers introduced Spanish Pointers to England.

1714 George I.

1715 Jacobite Rebellion.

1745 Second Jacobite Rebellion.

1758 *The Compleat Sportsman*, by Thomas Fairfax.

1760 George III. Shooting over pointers now the general custom.

1784 *A Tour of the Highlands*, by Colonel Thomas Thornton. Published in 1804, but extracted from game records at this date. The first account of shooting as practised in the north of England and Scotland. Extremely interesting.

1789 The Italian practice of 'posting guns round a cover' was noted as 'in general a very murderous practice'.

1790 *The British Sportsman*, by William Augustus Osbaldiston. An indiscriminate and massive copy of previous authors as far back as Markham and earlier. Hardly one original thought. Includes various points on shooting.

1801 *Sports and Pastimes of the People of England*, by Joseph Strutt. Encyclopaedic, from hunting to cards. Inaccurate. Little on shooting.
Rural Sports, by the Rev. William Barker Daniel. Four volumes without much order and full of anecdote, partly compiled while in Kings Bench debtors' prison. A fair amount on shooting.

1802 Peace of Amiens.

1804 *A Tour of France*, by Colonel Thomas Thornton. An account of his shooting and sport in France, where he made a tour during the Peace of Amiens. Racy and interesting.

1813 Percussion cap introduced.

1816 *Instructions to Young Sportsmen in all that relates to Guns and Shooting*, by Lt.-Col. Peter Hawker. A pioneer book on wild-fowling and punt-gunning. Numerous editions.

1818 *Anecdotes and History of Cranbourne Chase*, by the Rev. William Chafin. Interesting comments on the development of shooting over the previous century.

1820 George IV.

1830 William IV.

1831 Game Laws revised.

1837 Victoria.

1840 *An Encyclopedia of Rural Sports*, by D. Blaine. Encyclopaedic in content, but much copied from Hawker and others.

1845 *Wild Sports and Natural History of the Highlands*, by Charles St John. Among the first of the naturalist collector sportsmen. Numerous editions.

1854 Breechloader invented.

1855 *Manual of Rural Sports*, by Stonehenge (J. H. Walsh). Covers shooting and much revised in numerous editions.

1860 Widespread introduction of the breech loading shotgun and driven game shooting beginning to be practised. Several claims as to where started, but almost certainly East Anglia.

1865 First field trial held at Southill, Bedford.

1866 Osbaldiston, Squire of All England, wrote his *Memoirs*; edited by E. D. Cuming in 1926, they give a racy and vivid picture of the development of shooting in the nineteenth century.

1880 Ground Game Act.

1884 *Sport in the Highlands and Lowlands of Scotland*, by Tom Speedy. Gives the viewpoint of the Victorian sportsman to changing sport in this area during this period.

1885 *Sport*, by W. Bromley Davonport. Provides similar views on changes in England.

1889 The Badminton Library: *Moor and Marsh, Shooting, Field and Covert*, by Lord Walsingham and Sir R. Payne Gallwey. *The Art of Shooting*, by Charles Lancaster (13 editions).

1892 *Letters to Young Shooters*, Sir R. Payne Gallwey. Also author of *High Pheasants in Theory and Practice*. (An extremely dull pamphlet, barely a book, which proves nothing.)

1892 He edited Hawker's Diaries (reputedly taking considerable lib ties with them in the process). Also wrote a book on wildfowling which owes much to Hawker.

1894 *The Grouse*, by H. A. Macpherson and A. J. Stuart Wortley.

1896 *The Partridge*, by H. A. Macpherson and A. J. Stuart Wortley.

1901 Edward VII.

Kings of the Rod, Rifle and Gun, by Thormanby (J. Willmott Dixon). Shows development of shooting over nineteenth century.

1902 *The Pointer and his Predecessor*, by William Arkwright. A folio volume which also traces the development of shooting as a sport.

BIBLIOGRAPHY OF SOME BOOKS ON SHOOTING SINCE 1900

Alington, Charles	Partridge Shooting
Arnold, Richard	Pigeon Shooting
	The Shooter's Handbook
	The Shoreshooter
	Automatic and Repeating Shotguns
	Come Shooting With Me
Bacon, A. F. L.	Enchanted Days with Rod and Gun
Baker, Max	Sport with Wood Pigeons
Barclay, E. N.	Shooting for Beginners (S.T. Library)
Barton, F. T.	Pheasants in Covert and Aviary
	etc.
Beaven, T. P.	A Sportsman Looks Back
	A Sportsman's Fireside Memories
Bonnett, F.	The Shotgun and its Uses
	Mixed and Rough Shooting
Bower, J. G. (Klaxon)	Heather Mixture
Brander, Michael	Roughshooter's Dog
	Roughshooter's Sport
	Ground Game (S. T. Library)
	Gundogs: Their Care and Training
	Hunting and Shooting
	Training the Pointer–Retriever
	Sporting Pigeon Shooting
	etc.
Bratby, Michael	Grey Goose (illus. Peter Scott)
	Through the Air
Brown, A. R. H.	My Game Book
Burrard, Major Sir G.	In the Gunroom
	The Modern Shotgun (3 Volumes)
	etc.
Cadman, A.	Shouldergunning for Duck (S.T. Library)
	Goose Shooting (S.T. Library)
	etc.
Carey, Lewis	My Gun and I
Carlisle, G. L.	Shotgun Marksmanship (with Percy Stanbury)

238

Cazenove, B.	Grouse Shooting and Moor Management
Chalmers, Patrick R.	Field Sports of Scotland (Sportsman's Library)
	The Shooting Man's England
	Green Days and Blue Days
	The Frequent Gun
	Birds Ashore and Aforeshore
	At the Sign of the Dog and Gun
	A Peck o' Maut
	etc.
Chapel, C. E.	Field, Skeet and Trapshooting
Chapman, Abel	The Borders and Beyond
	Retrospect
	etc.
Churchill, Robert	How to Shoot
	Game Shooting
Clapham, Richard	The A.B.C. of Shooting
	Rough Shooting
	Sport on Fell, Beck and Tarn
	etc.
Coats, A. J.	The Amateur Keeper
	Pigeon Shooting
Coles, C. L.	Pigeon Shooting (S.T. Library)
Craig, C. W. Thurlow	Shooter's Delight
	etc.
Dawson, Major Kenneth	Letters to Young Sportsmen
	Just an Ordinary Shoot
	Marsh and Mudflat
	Son of a Gun
Day, J. Wentworth	Sporting Adventure
	The Modern Fowler
	The Dog in Sport
	King George V as a Sportsman
	The Modern Shooter
	etc.
Dewar, Douglas	Game Birds
	etc.
Dobie, G. W. M.	Winter and Rough Weather
	etc.
Drought, Capt. J. B.	A Shot in the Making
	Successful Shooting

Green Memory
Partridge Shooting (Sportsman's Library)

Duncan, Stanley The Complete Wildfowler (with G. Thorne)

Ellacott, S. E. Guns
etc.

Escritt, L. B. Rifle and Gun
etc.

Evans, Lt.-Col. G. P. Small-Game Shooting
Fisher, A. O. Exmoor and Other Days
Fitzgerald, B. Vesey British Game
etc.

Fitzgerald, Gerald Pot Luck
Fletcher, Henry The Sporting Scene
Come and Shoot

Gladstone, Sir Hugh Shooting with Surtees
Record Bags and Shooting Records
etc.

Goodwin, Gen. Sir J. Making a Shoot (Sportsman's Library)

Grattan, Gurney A. Rough Shooting
Hardy, Hon. A. E. G. Autumns in Argyll with Rod and Gun
My Happy Hunting Grounds

Hardy, Capt. H. F. H. English Sport
etc.

Harris, Clive History of the Birmingham Proof House

Harrison, Jeffery G. Pastures New
Hartley, G. W. Wild Sport and Some Stories
etc.

Hearn, Arthur Shooting and Gunfitting
Hipgrave, A. The Management of a Partridge Beat
Hutchinson, Horace Shooting
Hutchinson, H. G. British Sporting Birds (with F. B. Kirkman)

Imrie, David Lakeland Gamekeeper
The Keeper's Year (S.T. Library)
Johnson, A. E. B. Shooting Wood Pigeon
Jones, Owen The Sport of Shooting
Keith, E. C. Gun for Company
Shoots and Shooting

	A Countryman's Creed etc.
Leslie, A. S.	The Grouse in Health and Disease
Long, W. H. T.	The Gun in the Field
Lynn-Allen, E. H.	Rough Shoot
	Leaves from a Game Book
	The Way of a Gun
	A Partridge Year (with A. P. Robertson)
Macintyre, Dugald	Highland Gamekeeper
	Round the Seasons on a Grouse Moor
	Wild Life of the Highlands etc.
Mackie, Sir Peter	The Keeper's Book
Maxwell, Aymer	Partridges and Partridge Manors
	Pheasants and Covert Shooting
McCall, Ian	Your Shoot—Gamekeepering and Management
McClean, Colin	At Dawn and Dusk
Moxon, P. R. A.	Gundogs, Modern Methods of Training (S.T. Library)
Nichols, J. C. M.	Birds of Marsh and Mere
	Shooting Ways and Shooting Days
Page, R.	New Ways with Partridges
Parker, Eric	Partridges Yesterday and Today
	Elements of Shooting
	An Alphabet of Shooting
	Shooting Days
	The Shooting Week-end Book
	Game Pie
	Field River and Hill
	etc. Also editor Lonsdale Library
	Shooting by Moor, Field and Shore
	Game Birds, Beasts and Fishes
	The Keeper's Book
	Anthology of Sporting Prose & Verse
	Also editor of revised edition of Lt.-Col. P. Hawker's Diaries and his Instructions to Young Sportsmen
Pilkington, S. M.	With a Gun to the Hill
Pitchford, D. J. Watkins ('B.B.')	The Shooting Man's Bedside Book

	The Sportsman's Bedside Book
	Dark Estuary
	etc.
Pitman, Ian	And Clouds Flying
Pollard, Major H. B. C.	Game Birds and Game Bird Shooting
	The Rearing, Preservation and Shooting of Game Birds
	Shotguns, Their History & Development
	A History of Firearms
	etc.
Powell, Bill	The Grey Geese Call
Prichard, Major Hesketh	Sport in Wildest Britain
	etc.
Purdey, T. D. S.	The Shot Gun (with Captain J. A. Purdey (Sportsman's Library)
Richards, Coombe	Sporting Vacations
	High Birds and Low
	etc.
Roberts, E. L.	The Happy Countryman
Ross, R. E.	Wings over the Marshes
Scott, Lord George	Grouse Land and the Fringe of the Moor
	etc.
Scott, Peter	Wild Chorus
	Morning Flight
	etc.
Sedgwick, Noel M.	The Young Shot
	The Gun on Saltings and Stubble
	With Dog and Gun
	Wildfowling and Roughshooting
	By Covert, Field and Marsh
	A Shooting Man's Year
	Shooting Wildfowl and Game
	Shooting Round the Year
	Waders, Woodcock and Snipe (S.T. Library)
	etc.
Seigne, J. W.	Woodcock and (with E. O. Keith) Snipe (Sportsman's Library)
Sprake, Leslie	A Shooting Man's Calendar
	Perdix the Partridge

	Pheasant Shooting (Sportsman's Library)
Standfield, F. G.	Syndicate Shooting
	Pheasant Shooting (S.T. Library)
Stanford, J. K.	Full Moon at Sweatenham
	Mixed Bagmen
	The Twelfth
	The Wandering Gun
	Guns Wanted
	Partridge Shooting (S.T. Library)
	Grouse Shooting (S.T. Library)
	etc.
Stephens, Martin	Letters to Young Shooters
	Grouse Shooting (Sportsman's Library)
	etc.
Teasdale-Buckell, G. T.	The Complete Shot
Tegner, Henry	The Sporting Rifle
	etc.
Tennyson, Julian	Rough Shooting
Thomas, Gough	Shotguns and Cartridges (S.T. Library)
Thomas, William	Rabbit Shooting to Ferrets
Thompson, Harry V.	The Rabbit (with Alistair N. Worden)
Turner, T. W.	Memoirs of a Gamekeeper
Waddington, Richard	Grouse Shooting and Moor Management
	etc.
Walsingham, Lord	Hit and Miss
Whitaker, Peter H.	Approach to Shooting
	Rough Shooting (S.T. Library)
Willock, Colin	Duck Shooting
Winnall, R. N.	Shore Shooting
	Rough Shooting (with G. K. Yeates) (Sportsman's Library)